The Buy-to-Let Bible

Ajay Ahuja

The Buy-to-Let Bible
by Ajay Ahuja

Published by
Lawpack Publishing Limited
76-89 Alscot Road
London SE1 3AW

www.lawpack.co.uk

First edition 2002
Second edition 2003
    Reprinted twice

Exclusion of Liability and Disclaimer
Whilst every effort has been made to ensure that this **Lawpack** publication provides accurate and expert guidance, it is impossible to predict all the circumstances in which it may be used. Accordingly, neither the publisher, author, retailer, nor any other suppliers shall be liable to any person or entity with respect to any loss or damage caused or alleged to be caused by the information contained in or omitted from this **Lawpack** publication.

For convenience (and for no other reason) 'him', 'he' and 'his' has been used throughout and should be read to include 'her', 'she' and 'her'.

Contents

List of figures

List of tables

I dedicate this book to my mother.

Thanks to Anjana and Tom for their comments.
A special thanks to Ellie for her support and research.

About the author

Ajay Ahuja is the founder and owner of the national accountancy practice Accountants Direct. It is the first in the UK that deals exclusively with the provision of references for the self-employed for mortgaging purposes. This experience has led to an in-depth knowledge of mortgages and the property market in general.

He currently consults with various local councils and accommodation projects, attempts to provide innovative solutions to problems being faced by the homeless and comments on issues surrounding social housing.

He now owns and controls a property portfolio worth £3m and provides housing for more than 250 people around the UK.

Introduction

I started with nothing. I bought my first property when I was 24 with £500 and now, at the age of 31, I own 50 properties and earn an income in excess of £250,000 per annum. It's not difficult but it requires DEDICATION, PERSISTENCE and DISCIPLINE. If you lack any of the above, then forget it.

My dedication, persistence and discipline about being rich were not driven by money but by freedom - the freedom to do what I like, when I like, without worrying about my boss or my wallet. Freedom does not have to be your driving factor; it could be a brand new Ferrari or private schooling for your children. Whatever it is, it's this that will keep you going. With the right properties, financial products and tenants, there is no doubt you will succeed, and this book will show you how to go about finding the right properties, financial products, tenants and more.

So why choose property? Why not invest in stocks and shares? The first reason is that property carries an inherently low risk factor. Houses will not go out of fashion or become obsolete like services or products. They are an essential for us all. That's why house prices have consistently doubled every 10-15 years over the last century. Coupled with the fact that monthly rental values rise with wages (which is a function of inflation) and that the mortgage payment is relatively fixed (only altering with interest rate fluctuations), the profit element always rises. In addition, after the mortgage has been paid, the rent is all profit. That's why many people see investing in property as their pension fund.

The second reason is basic economics. With an expanding population, fragmenting families, an increasingly mobile workforce, fewer properties for sale and fewer council owned properties, THE DEMAND FOR RENTAL PROPERTIES EXCEEDS SUPPLY.

The third reason is an inherent attribute in all of us - we are lazy! To play the stock market properly requires lengthy research, ongoing monitoring and nerves of steel for the duration of the investment. That's why three out of four private investors lose money. When a property is set up properly, you just sit back and watch the money roll in.

I am a chartered accountant. I left employment when I was 27 to get into the property business and I must admit the training I received in accountancy and, more importantly in business has helped me in my success. However, the principles involved are not difficult to grasp. I bought my first property in 1996 for myself to live in, couldn't get used to it, and so let it out. I soon realised that the tenant was paying my mortgage as well as my beer money (about £120 per month), and it required minimal effort from me. I thought, 'This is easy!' so I bought another one and did the same. 48 properties later…you get the idea.

So whether you are thinking of creating a multi-million pound property empire or simply buying the house next door to earn a modest secondary income, this book is for you. But before you get pound signs in your eyes you have to ask yourself: Is property right for you? There are four key questions you have to ask yourself:

1. Can I budget well?
2. Do I like and am I capable of dealing with people from a range of backgrounds?
3. Do I like property?
4. Am I a responsible person?

1. Can I budget well?

Are you the type of person who spends their wages before they are earned? Do you often use your overdraft facility and credit cards to fund your lifestyle? Do you make impulse purchases on the high street and then regret them later? Do you wake up in the morning after an evening out and wonder how you managed to spend all of the £100 that was in your pocket the night before? If this sounds familiar then investing in property is currently not for you. Investing in property could be an option at a later date but your spending has to mature. A mortgage is a legal commitment to pay a sum of money on regular set dates and breach of this commitment can result in damage to your credit rating and could ultimately lead to bankruptcy.

Sometimes rent from several properties comes in cash on the same day. I might have £3,000 in cash in my pocket and it certainly gives you a feeling that you are £3,000 richer, but you are not! You've got to pay the mortgage, service charges, building insurance, etc. You have to be disciplined enough to bank the cash and not assume that all the rent is profit, which is surprisingly easy to forget.

2. Do I like and am I capable of dealing with people from a range of backgrounds?

The type of people you will be meeting with will be:

- **Tenants:** They can be of any age over 18, from any profession, male or female, from any race or religion. Have you got any hang-ups about a certain group of people?

- **Estate and Letting Agents:** Despite what people say about agents, my experience with them is that they conduct themselves in a professional manner. They can be a bit pushy sometimes, but you've got to expect that when dealing with people whose business depends on the sale or management of an asset worth many thousands of pounds. Are you easily persuaded? Can you stand your ground?

- **Solicitors:** Usually very intelligent people. Can you convince him of your intelligence so that he doesn't keep you in the dark when you want to know what's going on?

- **Lenders:** Your point of contact is normally a call centre operator. Are you able to keep your cool to extract the right information from the operator?

- **Mortgage Brokers:** Again, very sharp people. Can you keep up with his calculations? Are you asking the right questions?

3. Do I like property?

There is absolutely no point in getting involved in property if you are not interested in property. Any successful businessman will tell you that if you are thinking of starting a business, the first thing you've got to ask yourself is if you enjoy the business you are getting into. Do you believe in the product? Is the business you are contemplating something that your mind naturally wanders to? Is the line between work and pleasure blurred when it comes to looking at and maintaining property?

It is your interest in property that will ensure that you dedicate the correct amount of time in order for your property business to succeed.

4. Am I a responsible person?

You have many legal obligations to your tenant, lender and letting agent. Property is a serious business. You have to be aware of these obligations and be prepared to fulfil them. Failure to do so can have serious repercussions, including jail!

Well, is property for you?

If you can answer 'Yes' to three out of four of those questions, then you are basically ready for property investment. To be really good, though, you need to work on the question you answered 'No' to. If you answered 'Yes' to all questions, then there is nothing to stop you from becoming a millionaire within the next 10 years, and that is fact. The most common type of business in the last 50 years that made people millionaires is either commercial or residential property.

The formula

The formula detailed below is the formula that has made me a millionaire in five years. The same formula has created many millionaires - it is nothing groundbreaking or original.

Property is inherently a long-term path to wealth - that is the nature of property. If you have the patience to play the property market, you will make money. I have to admit that my rapid acquisition in wealth is partly due to the property boom since 1996, but it is also adhering to the principles I stuck to, detailed in this book.

The formula is simple

- **Find the initial investment:** Starting a business requires some initial capital; but getting into the property game is not as expensive as you may think. It is possible to start with nothing! Chapter 1 deals with identifying your attitude to risk and inventive ways of raising your initial investment in order for you to purchase your first property. Once you've raised the initial investment, you can progress to finding the right lender to finance the property you wish to buy.

- **Find the right lender:** In chapter 2 you will create a profile most suited to your personal circumstances and attitudes in order to find the right lender for you.

- **Find the right property:** From chapter 3 you will be able to identify easily properties that can give you a significant return on your investment. You will be taught what to look for when looking for a property, making an offer, how to identify properties with returns in excess of 25 per cent and whether or not to refurbish.

- **Find the right tenant:** Finding the right tenant is key to the success of your investment. In chapter 4 you will identify what tenant is best for your property, you and your lender and where to advertise. Chapter 4 will examine the benefits of credit checking, relationships between landlord and tenant, and rent collection.

- **How to create and expand your portfolio:** How to own a multitude of properties by the secret of remortgaging and to keep your portfolio by adopting risk management techniques. Check out chapter 5.

- **Minimise tax:** Chapter 6 deals with how to avoid (but not evade!) tax in connection with property.

- **Operate legally:** Chapter 7 deals with all the legal aspects a landlord might face when investing in property. It covers the types of contracts you will enter into, the regulations governing residential letting property and the law in general.

- **Essential references:** Chapter 8 is a one-stop shop of all the addresses, phone numbers and websites that relate to investing in property. This includes, amongst others, hotspot areas to invest in, lenders, insurers and accommodation projects.

1 The initial investment

So, to become a professional landlord you need bundles of cash – false! A portfolio can be amassed from nothing or as little as £500, as I did five years ago. We have access to cash reserves that we do not even know about because we are not fully aware of certain financial products on the market.

The term 'initial investment' implies that starting capital is required. However, even though it is advisable to have an initial investment, it is not mandatory in order to set up a multi-million-pound investment portfolio – no matter what business experts say. I'm sure you've heard many testimonies of multi-millionaires who started with a couple of pounds in their pocket. What made these people succeed was their attitude to risk. To become a millionaire in business you have to take a certain degree of risk. Otherwise, we would all be rich! However, I expect that many readers do not have the same attitudes to risk as the millionaires I have just mentioned. The beauty of property is that you can invest in property according to your own personal attitudes to risk.

Let's look at the risks in investing in property. There are three core elements making up the income and expenditure account – income being rent, expenditure being the mortgage payment and maintenance. All these three elements can be fixed if need be, and as long as income exceeds expenditure, you're in the money!

That's right – guaranteed profit. There are financial products out there that can guarantee rental income, fix mortgage payments and fix maintenance expenditure. Consider which risk class you fit in, based on the table below:

Risk class	Income	Expenditure	
	Rent	Mortgage Cost	Maintenance Cost
1	Guaranteed	Nil	Fixed

If only! This is the investor who has enough cash to buy a property outright, guarantee his income, never worry about maintaining the property and still earns treble what a bank or building society will offer him.

Risk class	Income	Expenditure	
2	Guaranteed	Fixed	Fixed

This is the investor who does not have bundles of cash but is willing to borrow. However, he also wants to ensure that he will meet his mortgage payment and any maintenance costs. This is someone who is risk-averse and is not typically a handyman when it comes to household repairs.

Risk class	Income	Expenditure	
3	Guaranteed	Fixed	Variable

This is a risk-averse investor, but he can do his own household repairs or is willing to take the risk on household repairs.

Risk class	Income	Expenditure	
4	Guaranteed	Variable	Variable

This is an investor who accepts a fair degree of risk to interest rate fluctuations and household repairs.

Risk class	Income		Expenditure	
	Rent	Mortgage Cost	Maintenance Cost	
5	Not Guaranteed	Fixed	Fixed	

This is an investor who probably works and earns more than he spends in order to cover the mortgage and maintenance payments. Receipt of rental income is crucial, but not crucial enough to meet the fixed mortgage and maintenance payments on time. Cashflow is not an issue for this investor in the short term.

6	Not Guaranteed	Fixed	Variable

Again this is an investor who works and earns more than he spends. However, he is also willing to take the risk of maintaining the property because he is a handyman or is just simply willing to take the risk.

7	Not Guaranteed	Variable	Variable

The risk taker. Here we have our future millionaire. His income is maximised because he obtains his rent in the open market, his mortgage payment is minimised because he sources the best-discounted mortgage product and he has taken full risk on maintenance hoping that nothing major will go wrong. This strategy is probably suited to investors who comfortably earn an income in excess of their spending. Cashflow is crucial.

Table 1.1. Risk classes

There are other permutations of the above model but most people fall into one of the seven categories. The higher the risk factor you are, the more money you can make, but the key factor is whichever risk factor you are, you will make money.

The initial investment you require is completely determined by your attitude to risk. The lower your risk factor, the higher the initial investment will be. For example, an investor who falls into risk class 1 has to finance the whole purchase price of the property in order for him not to have to meet a monthly mortgage payment. Hence, he is not dependent on the punctuality of the tenants' rent payment; this way his investment in the property market is restricted to his savings in the bank. On the other hand, someone with a risk factor 7, with nothing in the bank, can borrow on an unsecured personal loan basis. He can then use this as deposits for a number of properties on a buy-to-let mortgage scheme and acquire a number of properties.

Let's look at a specific example:

Mandy with risk class 1 and £40,000 to invest

Mandy buys a property for £40,000 in Northampton. (Yes, £40,000! There are over 300 hotspots listed in the reference chapter where properties are regularly advertised for £40,000 or less.) She guarantees her rent from a rental guarantee company (see chapter 8), borrows nothing and pays for a maintenance insurance contract which covers the cost for all major incidental maintenance expenditure. Her monthly return is:

	£
Rent	450
Mortgage	0
Maintenance	25
Profit	425

Arnie with risk class 7 and £3,000 to invest

Arnie borrows £18,000 on an unsecured basis at 8 per cent APR over seven years and uses this to fund three properties for £40,000 each in Northampton on a buy-to-let mortgage basis at 85 per cent 'loan to value' at 6 per cent APR. This means that he has to put down £6,000 each on the three properties. This adds up to £18,000 unsecured borrowings. The £3,000 that Arnie has goes towards professional fees on all three properties.

	1	2	3	Total £
Rent	500	500	500	1,500
Mortgage (interest only)	170	170	170	510
Unsecured Loan (interest only)	120	120	120	360
Maintenance	0	25	50	75
Profit	210	185	160	555

Arnie earns more than Mandy but Arnie has a greater borrowing requirement. Currently this proves the principle that BORROWING IS CHEAP.

The reason for this is because the returns to be made from property are far greater than the cost of borrowing. Typically the return from property is around 20 per cent and the cost of borrowing is around six per cent at current rates. This assumes that you have chosen the right property, which this book shows you how to do in chapter 3.

Taking this example further let's say property prices increase by 10 per cent over three years. Then the total profit made by each investor by way of rental profit and capital appreciation profit over the three years is:

	Mandy (Risk Factor 1) £	Arnie (Risk Factor 7) £
Rental Profit (36 months x monthly rental profit)	15,300	19,980
Capital Appreciation (10% x total cost of properties bought)	4,000	12,000
Total	**19,300**	**31,980**

Comparing these two investors shows that Arnie who started with £3,000 has earned 66 per cent more than Mandy who started with £40,000! Looking at the actual return from your initial investment being:

$$\frac{\text{Profit} \times 100}{\text{Initial investment}}$$

Then the returns for each investor are as follows:

	Mandy (Risk Factor 1)	Arnie (Risk Factor 7)
Total profit (from the table above)	19,300	31,980
Initial investment	40,000	3,000
Return on initial investment over 3 years	48%	1,066%

	Mandy (Risk Factor 1)	Arnie (Risk Factor 7)
Return on initial investment averaged over 1 year	16%	355%
Return on initial investment if deposited in a high interest building society account (current Bank of England base interest rate)	5%	5%

You can see that both investors have made returns in excess of any high interest building society account. You can also see that Arnie has made phenomenal returns far in excess of most investment funds or even technology stocks at their peak. The best thing is that you are investing in property, which all of us have some degree of understanding in, rather than a stock which you know little about and have to rely heavily on the financial press and tipsters.

But an even more important principle than the one above is that WHATEVER YOUR ATTITUDE TO RISK IS, YOU WILL MAKE MONEY!

The reality is that in the last three years we have seen average property prices grow by 10 per cent every year rather than 10 per cent over three years. This equates to 33 per cent capital appreciation over the three years. Thus the annual return from property over the last three years for both investors was 24 per cent and 662 per cent respectively. This example gives you an indication of how I have amassed great

wealth through property, as any money invested has grown by over six times each year because I have a risk factor of 7. So every £1,000 I invested was worth £6,620 in year 1, £13,240 in year 2 and £19,860 in year 3.

In the reference chapter you will find all the providers for guaranteed rent, buy-to-let mortgages and maintenance insurers and contractors.

Now, whatever risk factor you are, this will determine how much initial investment is needed. Assuming a property is at a purchase price of £50,000, the following initial investment will be needed:

Risk Factor	Initial Investment (£)
1	51,000
2-5	8,500-50,999
6	1,000
7	Nil

This assumes a 15 per cent deposit for the mortgage and £1,000 fees for solicitors, valuations and the initial void period when waiting to find the right tenant. Risk factor 6 investors borrow the initial deposit and risk factor 7 investors borrow the initial deposit and associated fees by way of secured or unsecured borrowings.

Raising the initial investment

So you've decided which risk factor you are and this has determined how much initial investment is required. How do you then go about raising the initial investment? The following table ranks, in order, the 'cost' to you, starting with the cheapest first, the cost being the effective interest rate being paid on the initial investment as a result of your choice of investing in property. BOE means current Bank of England base rate.

Source	Cost	Narrative
Personal assets	0%	Assets that are no longer being used but have some resale value. This may be jewellery, cars, furniture, pieces of art, electrical equipment, etc. The cost is nil as the assets are not being used but they could be used to realise some cash in order to invest. Look in the garage or attic – you may be surprised! Think about it like this – you're trading in your Ford now for the Ferrari in five years' time!
Savings	BOE Base Rate	You may have savings in a deposit account or cash ISA. If you use this money the cost will be the lost interest that would have been earned if you had left it in the account.
Endowment policies or company shares	BOE Base Rate + 3%	You could surrender an endowment policy or liquidise a current share portfolio to raise the cash. I recommend you talk to your financial adviser and stockbroker before taking this action as you could be better off holding out on some

Source	Cost	Narrative
		of these policies or shares. But it could be time to let go of some poorly performing stocks and enter the property arena as so many of the share market investors are doing now. The cost of this on average is equivalent to the average return the stock market delivers. This, of course, will be different depending on the type of policy or stocks you hold.
Borrow from family	BOE +4%	You may have a family member who has cash sitting in the bank and is willing to lend it to you. You can offer them a better rate of return than any deposit account could. If he is a close member of the family they may lend it to you for 0%, but if you proposition a family member offering BOE+4% you might get quite a few more positive responses than expected. You could access your inheritance early, as many families do, to avoid inheritance tax. As long as the donator lives seven years beyond the date of the gift there is no inheritance tax to pay and is thus beneficial to

Source	Cost	Narrative	Source	Cost	Narrative
		both parties. A family member may be more willing to give you assets if you are proposing to invest it further, rather than to just simply squander it on a new car or holiday.			on your current credit card and then apply for a credit card that has a low introductory rate for balance transfers until the balance is cleared. Once your new credit card has been approved, you transfer your existing balance on your old credit card to the new credit card at the introductory rate, typically BOE+2%. This rate is fixed until you clear the balance. You may, however, not get this new credit card. The other way is to draw down the cash on your existing credit card at the credit card rate. This can be expensive, but if the property you have found has a high income yield you could use the cash on a short-term basis, say one to two years, and use the profits to clear the credit card balance. You may be able to arrange an overdraft with your bank or a personal loan at around BOE+6%. You need to speak to your bank manager. You can also go to other unsecured lenders, but there are high arrangement fees and the interest rate can even go up to BOE+35%! You need to shop around, but I
Secured borrowings	BOE +2-7%	To do this, you must already own a property. The cheapest way to do this is to remortgage the whole property and release the equity tied up in your home. It pays to shop around. A good mortgage broker could probably beat the current rate that you are paying now and even reduce your monthly payments whilst still raising you some cash on top. The other way is to get a second charge loan where you keep your existing mortgage and borrow on the remaining equity on the house. You've probably seen the TV ads promising you a new car or holiday just from one phone call. Well, forget a new car or holiday – we're going property hunting!			
Unsecured borrowings	BOE +2-15%	The cheapest way to do this is by transferring a current credit card balance to a new credit card with introductory rate offers. You draw out as much cash as you can			

Source	Cost	Narrative
		would advise steering clear of anything with an interest rate higher than 25% unless you are really desperate and the property you have found has a very high income yield.
Get a partner	Dependent	The other way to raise the cash is by taking on a financial partner. This means that the financial risk is borne by the partner, but you end up doing all the work. The partner will be entitled to a share of your profits and you will not be free to do what you want with the property. Equating the cost to you will depend on how successful the property is, as the cost will be the share of profits made. Even though this is the most expensive way to finance a property business, it can also be the cheapest way if the whole project fails as your partner has taken the full financial risk. If this is the only method you can use to get into property, I would still advise taking on a partner as you will still be participating in a share of the property market.

Table 1.2. Raising the initial investment

The above table is not an exhaustive list. You may have other good ideas for raising finance, but if you can't raise the finance the project can't go ahead; it's as simple as that. The only other way is to change your attitude to risk. This means being willing to take a bigger risk and hence increase your risk factor thus reducing the initial investment needed. Greater borrowings will be inevitable.

I raised my initial investment by saving as much of my salary as I could. While my colleagues were spending everything they earned on high rents on apartments, expensive holidays and designer clothes I saved my money by living in one room in a shared house, holidaying in the UK and wearing unbranded clothes. After five years I live in a large detached house with swimming pool, holiday abroad three times a year and wear only designer clothes. You need patience and a medium- to long-term vision if you truly desire to have enough wealth to live the lifestyle you want.

If all else fails

If you are struggling to find the initial investment there are still three further tricks you could consider:

1. Get a 100 per cent loan-to-value residential mortgage
2. Create a vendor deposit
3. Get cashback on completion

Get a 100 per cent loan to value residential mortgage

There is still one way you can acquire a property if you are a first time buyer. There are certain lenders that provide 100 per cent residential mortgages that are free of fees. This means the lender funds the whole purchase of the property and pays for all the valuation and solicitor fees.

This product is for residential purposes only. However, you can make the application with the intent to live in the property but then inform the lender when the purchase completes that you intend to let it out now as you have changed your mind. Some lenders don't mind and simply charge a letting fee of £50-£100 per year. Some lenders, usually building societies, charge additional interest, typically two per cent, on the loan. You have to look at your figures very carefully to ensure the rent can cover the 100 per cent financing plus the additional interest if need be.

A list of 100 per cent fee-free lenders can be found in the reference chapter.

Create a vendor deposit

This is where you basically get the vendor to pay your deposit! This is best explained by following the example below:

Gavin wishes to buy an investment property for, say, £54,000, but he only has £3,000 to invest. The minimum deposit he needs is 15 per cent of £54,000, which equals £8,100. You may think he cannot go ahead as he has a shortfall of £5,100.

However, if he got the vendor to inflate the purchase price to £60,000, then the deposit required is 15 per cent of £60,000, which equals £9,000. If he also got the vendor to contribute £6,000 and Gavin contributed £3,000, with the total contribution being

£9,000, then Gavin can purchase the property.

This can best be shown by the following table:

	Without Vendor Deposit £	With Vendor Deposit £
Purchase price	54,000	60,000
Deposit required (assume 15% of purchase price)	8,100	9,000
Gavin's actual investment	3,000	3,000
Shortfall of investment = Deposit required minus Gavin's actual investment	5,100	6,000
Vendor contribution = Inflated purchase price minus purchase price	N/A	6,000
Actual shortfall = Shortfall of investment minus vendor contribution	5,100	Nil

Here, the vendor gets:

£60,000 - £6,000 = £54,000

The inflated price - vendor contribution = original asking price

Gavin gets an investment property costing £54,000 for £3,000 initial investment and manages to increase the amount he can borrow from the mortgage lender. His borrowings are now greater than 85% loan to value as he now has borrowed 85% of £60,000. Everybody's a winner.

This trick is completely legal, but relies on the property being valued at a higher figure. This is likely because of three reasons:

- **Valuers do not like to down-value a property**, unless there is something wrong with it! If they think the purchase price is only slightly higher than what it is worth they will always value it at the purchase price. This is because the valuer knows that valuations are not an exact science. Valuations are based on what people will pay for a property and he will assume that if you are willing to pay, say, £60,000 then the property is probably worth £60,000. A 10 per cent gross inflation of the purchase price is not a lot considering you are only talking about an inflation of £6,000. For higher value properties (greater than £200,000) I would suggest a five per cent vendor deposit contribution as a £10,000 purchase price inflation could be contested.

- **You may be getting a bargain property**, i.e. the property is worth £60,000 but you are actually getting it for £54,000, hence it values up to £60,000.

- **Valuers are under pressure to value properties at the purchase price.** Lenders make money by lending money. If they instruct a firm of valuers that keep on down-valuing properties, then it becomes difficult for the lender to lend and hence make money. The more the valuer values property at the purchase price, the more money the lender makes. Especially in the current rising property price conditions, even if the valuer thinks that the purchase price is one per cent or two per cent inflated, he will assume that it will reach the valuation in a few months anyway.

There are tax issues. The vendor has to declare the inflated sales price to the Inland Revenue and thus will have to pay more Capital Gains Tax as his gain is deemed to be higher. For the vendor this may not be a problem as the Inland Revenue gives you an allowance in excess of £7,000 for a capital gain. If this inflated price does not take the gain above this allowance, then there is no increased Capital Gains Tax to pay.

Get cashback on completion

This is similar to creating a vendor deposit as it requires the property to be valued higher than the agreed price. You see cashback on completion offered by some car dealers on new cars when you take out finance on a new car. It is effectively a discount on the sales price.

Cashback on completion means exactly what it says. You receive cashback when you complete the transaction.

Let me use the same example as the one in 'Create a vendor deposit' to explain this. Assume that Gavin wants to buy a property at £54,000 and he only has £3,000 to invest. Let's assume the vendor agrees to sell the property at £60,000 with £6,000 cashback:

	Without Cashback £	With Cashback £
Purchase price	54,000	60,000
Deposit required (assume 15% of purchase price)	(8,100)	(9,000)
Deposit paid on exchange of contracts (assume 5%)	2,700	3,000
Deposit required to complete (remaining 10%)	5,400	6,000
Amount left to invest = £3,000 minus deposit paid on exchange	300	Nil
Shortfall = Deposit required to complete minus amount left to invest	5,100	6,000
Cashback	nil	6,000
Actual shortfall = Shortfall minus cashback	5,100	Nil

Here, the vendor gets his asking price of £54,000 which is the inflated price minus the cashback:

£60,000 - £6,000 = £54,000

and Gavin gets an investment property costing £54,000 with £3,000 initial investment.

The same rules apply to upward valuation and Capital Gains Tax mentioned above.

2 Finding the right buy-to-let mortgage provider

If you are funding the whole purchase of the property yourself then you can skip this chapter, as it deals with obtaining further borrowings to finance the property purchase.

A buy-to-let mortgage is a relatively new financial product, emerging onto the market in 1995, which allows anybody to purchase a house or flat with the intention of letting it out. This product allows you to borrow the finance needed to buy a property based on the rental income generated rather than on your actual personal income. Typically, as long as the rental income is greater than 130 per cent of the interest payment you could purchase the property, but this of course can vary depending on your mortgage.

For a buy-to-let mortgage, you typically need 15-25 per cent of the purchase price as a deposit, so for a £40,000 purchase price you would need between £6,000 and £10,000 and the lender would fund the other £30,000 to £34,000. A higher deposit is needed in comparison to a residential property, where the deposit needed is typically 0-10 per cent, as with a buy-to-let mortgage the property is not owner-occupied and the lender's mortgage payment depends on a suitable and reliable tenant being found. Hence this presents a higher risk to the lender. If they ever had to repossess the property, they would only need to achieve 85 per cent of the purchase price. This may only be the true market value of the property after it has been tenanted or if there is a property slump at the time of repossession.

What's best for you?

The most suitable buy-to-let mortgage for you depends on the following factors:

1. Your initial investment
2. The purchase price
3. The type of property
4. Your personal credit history
5. Your attitude to risk
6. The degree of aftercare
7. Duration of borrowing and maximising cashflow

Your initial investment

The initial investment dictates the maximum purchase price. This is best explained in an example:

Investor A has £7,000 to invest. He assumes £1,000 for professional fees and the initial void period, leaving a £6,000 deposit. Considering that the maximum loan to value (LTV) is 85 per cent, the greatest purchase price is:

£6,000/0.15 = £40,000

The maximum he can borrow is therefore £34,000. So the following formula holds:

$$\frac{\text{(Initial investment - professional fees)} = \text{maximum purchase price}}{\text{Deposit required}/100}$$

It is crucial to calculate the maximum purchase price so you know what you can afford to buy. There is no point looking at a property that is in excess of this maximum as no lender will lend in excess of 85 per cent LTV. It is also important to ensure your maximum purchase price is in excess of the lender's minimum purchase price – see below.

The purchase price

Almost all lenders have a minimum purchase price. The minimum purchase price starts at £6,500 and rises up to £75,000 for certain lenders. If your purchase price is below their minimum purchase price then the lender will not consider you under any circumstances. So the purchase price can dictate the mortgage you can get.

The type of property

Lenders have certain exclusions based on the type of property it is. The key exclusions are:

1. **Studio flats:** These are flats that have one main room that is used as a lounge and bedroom, plus a kitchen and a bathroom. They are excluded, as they can be difficult to sell if there was a property price slump.

2. **Ex-local authority houses and flats:** These are properties that were once owned by the local council and subsequently sold on to private people. They are excluded, as they are associated with the lower end of the property market.

3. **Flats above commercial properties:** These are excluded as the commercial property below could be let out to an Indian or Chinese take-away at some later date. Because of the smell of the food it would lead to a decline in the market value of the property.

4. **Flats with more than four storeys:** These will be considered a high-rise block and at the lower end of the property market.

5. **Multiple-title properties:** These are properties where a freehold exists with a number of long leases and you are trying to buy the freehold. An example of this is a block of flats.

6. **Non-standard construction:** If a house is not built of brick or does not have a pitched tile roof, it is deemed non-standard. For example, some houses may be constructed from poured concrete. Despite being perfectly fine houses, lenders may consider these properties inferior to standard construction properties.

The type of property can dictate the mortgage you can get.

Your personal credit history

What the lender is trying to establish is: are you a good bet? They will need to know that they will get back their money plus interest, with the minimum of effort. They will need to establish whether you are creditworthy.

There are two main credit reference agencies that all lenders consult before they make any lending decision: Experian and Equifax. They record a number of details about you based on your current and previous addresses in the last three years, namely:

1. **Electoral roll:** Details of whether you are on the electoral roll; some lenders require you to be on it before they can lend.

2. **County Court Judgments (CCJs):** These arise when a debtor has taken you to court to enforce payment of a debt and the debtor won the case. The court holds this information for six years from the date of the judgment. They also record if you subsequently paid the judgement.

3. **Individual Voluntary Arrangements (IVAs):** This is where you have become bankrupt and unable to pay your debts. Once you have been made bankrupt and the debts have been settled then you become a discharged bankrupt. Only once you have been discharged can you have any hope of obtaining credit again. You are automatically discharged after six years.

4. **Credit accounts:** These are all your loan accounts that have been active in the last six years and whether you have ever defaulted on them. Typical accounts are your mortgage account, credit and store card accounts and personal loans.

5. **Repossessions:** Details of any repossessions of your homes that have ever occurred.

6. **Previous searches:** These are previous credit searches by other lenders that you have made a credit application with.

7. **Gone Away Information Network (GAIN):** This is where you have moved home and not forwarded on the new address and not satisfied the debt.

8. **Credit Industry Fraud Avoidance System (CIFAS):** This is where the lender suspects fraud and just flags it up; you cannot be refused credit based on a suspicion.

Your credit file dictates the mortgage you can get. The key factors are CCJs or defaults. If you have any CCJs or defaults (points 2 & 4 above) you will be restricted to adverse credit lenders who charge higher arrangement fees and interest rates. If you have an IVA, repossession or GAIN on your file it is unlikely you will get a buy-to-let mortgage, but you will still probably be able to get a residential mortgage depending on when you had debt problems. It is worth noting that the buy-to-let mortgage market is further developing and a suitable product may come on to the market soon.

There is one key thing you should remember when filling out your form – do not lie! If lenders find out, they will demand repayment in full and they could inform the police of fraud – the charge being obtaining finance by deception. The credit reference agencies are becoming more and more sophisticated. They log every bit of information you put on every credit application and if you submit an application that was slightly different from a previous application, they will flag it up.

Your attitude to risk

As discussed earlier, your attitude to risk is key to the level of exposure you want to have over events that are out of your control. When it comes to mortgages, the only real risk is the interest rate. There are only two categories of type of interest rate – fixed or variable. There are various sub-categories of this in the table below:

Type		Narrative
Fixed	Fixed	This is for the low risk-taker. It ensures that the monthly mortgage payment is fixed for a period of time, usually between 1 and 10 years.
	Capped	This is also for a low risk-taker. It ensures that the mortgage payment never exceeds a certain amount but if interest rates fall then your mortgage payment can fall. No downside risk and only upside potential!
Variable	Tracker	This is where the interest rate being charged follows the exact rate being set by the Bank of England + a buy-to-let interest loading, typically 1-2%. You are fully exposed to the Bank of England interest rate fluctuations.
	Discount	This is where the initial interest rate is discounted by 1-4% for a specified period of time. This could be a discount on a tracker or a standard variable rate.

Type	Narrative
	You are exposed, but because there is a discount in place you don't feel the fluctuations quite as badly.
Stepped	This is where the discount is reduced over a number of years. So you would be entitled to a 3% discount in year 1, 2% discount in year 2 and 1% discount in year 3 for example.
Variable	This is just the standard variable rate set by the lender. Your mortgage payments are fully exposed to interest rate fluctuations.

Table 2.1. Types of interest rate

You have to be careful of the tie-in/lock-in periods that may exist with all these products. These are the minimum periods that you have to remain with the lender without incurring financial penalties if you wish to redeem the loan because you want to sell or remortgage the property.

Some lenders provide all the mortgages above and some lenders only provide some of these mortgages. The type of mortgage you want dictates the lender you have to approach.

The degree of aftercare

Some people require face-to-face contact with their lender. If this is so, then you can really only approach high street banks and building societies. There are many lenders who do not talk to the public and only liaise with your mortgage broker. Personally, I don't mind not having face-to-face contact, as my mortgage broker is quite efficient in handling my queries.

Duration of borrowing and maximising cashflow

The duration of the loan needs to meet your own personal criteria. This depends on your age, personal goals and cashflow. You may wish to own the property outright by a certain age. This means that you require a mortgage that is less than the normal 25-year period or a flexible mortgage where the interest is charged daily and can be settled whenever you want.

You may require an interest only mortgage rather than a repayment mortgage, so that your monthly payments are lower. This will maximise your cashflow. Not all lenders provide flexible or interest only mortgages, so if this is what you require it will limit your choice.

Typical profile

So after considering the seven factors dictating the type of mortgage you can get, you can build a profile that looks like this:

Factor	Profile
Maximum purchase price	£50,000
The purchase price	£45,000
The type of property	Private one-bedroom flat standard construction

Factor	Profile
Your personal credit history	Clean
Fixed or variable?	Fixed capped (no lock-in period)
The degree of aftercare	High street bank or building society
Duration of borrowing and maximising cashflow	25 years & interest only

With this profile you can approach a mortgage broker and he will be able to source a lender that meets your profile. I would advise that you make an application with a lender before you find the property, so that when you do find a property you can act quickly if need be.

3 Finding the right property

So you've got the finance in place, now you need to find the property. This is the most important decision in the whole process. It is the property you choose that dictates your success. There are many properties on the market but less than one per cent are worth buying.

During the whole property investment process there is only one figure you can ever be in control of: the purchase price. If the price is too high, then you can walk away. You only ever become involved in the whole property purchase process when the price is right. But what is the right price?

There is a rule of thumb that I always apply when looking for a property to invest in – I call it 'the rule of 12'. It's very simple to remember when looking at properties.

Let's assume the purchase price is £45,000. Knock off the two zeros at the end (in effect, divide the purchase price by 100) and you arrive at £450. This then determines the monthly rental figure that needs to be charged to obtain a 12 per cent gross yield. Gross yield is defined as:

$$\frac{\text{Annual rental income} \times 100}{\text{Property purchase price}} = \text{gross yield}$$

If you can achieve a 12 per cent yield, then go for it! Speak to letting agents or look in the local press for typical rental values for the area that you are looking at. This yield

is also stated as a payback period – the length of time it would take to own the property if you reinvested all the income earned to replenish your savings. You would calculate it as follows:

$$\frac{1}{\text{Gross yield}/100} = \text{payback period}$$

So in this example the payback period would be 8.33 years.

12 per cent is a like-for-like comparison to a bank or building society rate. So if your bank is offering four per cent you know that you can earn three times as much from investing in property. But this assumes that you have funded the whole property purchase out of your own funds. Usually this is not the case. When you borrow to finance the purchase, the returns are significantly higher as highlighted in the previous chapter.

When you become familiar with an area and its rental values, then you know when a property is a bargain. If typical rental values for a one-bedroom flat are £500 per month, then you instantly know if you walk past an agent's window and there's a flat advertised for £46,000, that you are going to get in excess of 12 per cent so it's worth an enquiry.

If, however, flats in the area are rarely priced under £70,000, then forget that area! You are not going to make any money there. It is the price that will dictate the area. Forget location, location, location; it's PRICE, PRICE, PRICE! This is because you are looking for a property to invest in rather that to live in.

It's surprisingly easy to manage a property outside your area once the property is set up right. There are many areas that offer you a return of 12 per cent and greater. Areas like these I call hotspots. In the reference chapter is a list of all the hotspots I have identified with their gross yields of 12 per cent and greater.

What about capital appreciation?

Capital appreciation is the amount the property rises in value over time. I never include the gains by capital appreciation in my calculation of yields because it is an unknown figure at the point you make the investment. If there were any certainty of the capital appreciation of a property then the purchase price of the property would include this gain. As there is a lot of uncertainty over capital appreciation because of the numerous variables involved, it is very difficult to predict when house prices will rise. Remember, the gain is only realised when you sell the property and the difficult thing with any investment is knowing when to get out and sell.

I see capital appreciation as a bonus. I focus on the investment as it stands. If it makes money now it will almost certainly make you money in the future. If the property prices crash, who cares! You are still making

money as the rent rises with inflation and the mortgage payment is still the same. If property prices soar, great! You can realise that equity by remortgaging or by selling and buying further properties! This way there is no downside risk and only upside potential.

Admittedly, there is a lot of money to be made in capital appreciation speculation, but this should be left to the professional property investors. They have the time to research the market and can stomach the loss if there is a property price crash.

How to achieve a higher return of 12 per cent

I have a property in Harlow, Essex that is a five-bedroom, two-bathroom property. I used to let it out to a large family – husband, wife and seven children! I was achieving around 12 per cent return and I was quite happy. I thought they would stay there for a long time, as there is a real shortage of five-bedroomed properties to rent, let alone buy. However, in business nothing is guaranteed and they decided to move out. So I readvertised the property and an 'accommodation project' approached me.

An accommodation project is a non-profit organisation, usually a charity or local government-funded body, that assists the homeless in the town or city in which they are based. They suggested to me that they would like to convert the property into five single units for people on housing benefit and they would handle the management for no charge. The conversion costs were minimal, simply installing independent locks on the door, providing cheap single beds in each room and basic kitchen appliances.

They said I would be able to charge on average £70 per week for each room, which equated to £1,515 per calendar month. I compared this to what I was originally getting of £600 per month and thought I should give it a go. I had to pay all the utility bills and council tax, but even after that my net profit was set to increase fivefold. I've been running this scheme for over a year now and I have never looked back. I even converted another one of my two-bedroom properties into a three-bedroomed place (converting the living room into another bedroom) to cash in on such a scheme.

It has not been without problems, though. The five-bedroom place is let to five guys of all ages and they can be quite boisterous. I have had complaints from the neighbours and environmental health but they haven't closed me down yet. The property requires more time and effort, but that is expected considering the high yield that one is obtaining.

If you consider this type of property, go for a property that can have four lettable rooms. This could be a four-bedroom property, or a three-bedroom two-reception property (converting one reception room into another bedroom) and see if you can get two bathrooms (even if one of the bathrooms is a shower room). I would set the yield required at 33 per cent. This means that you would need £20,000 rental income for a purchase price of £60,000.

For example, if the property had five rooms then you would require an average room rate of £77 per room (£20,000/52 weeks/five rooms).

Expect to visit this property every fortnight to make sure nothing has been damaged or there are no other people staying round other than the tenants. Also, remember that, legally, letting a property as individual rooms binds you to the Houses in Multiple Occupation Bill, which includes legal and management requirements regarding a licensing scheme and energy efficiency.

A list of accommodation projects can be found in the reference chapter. I would suggest you speak to them before entering into a venture, as they will be able to assess the likely demand and typical room rates.

Refurbishment

Should you refurbish a property? If you are new to the property game I would advise you not to. It is time-consuming, easy to be conned by builders, stressful and you lose money while the property is unlet. When viewing a prospective property, if it has had the kitchen or bathroom ripped out, forget it. By the time you have refurbished it you would have spent at least £5,000 in repair costs and interest and you would have built up an affection for the property. It will take you a long time to recoup the money and because you have invested a lot of your time on the property you may be too choosy over the right tenant to move in. I mean, do you really want to be sacrificing your evenings and weekends refurbishing a wreck? No! You want to be on the high street spending all that money you're earning from making the right property investments.

If you are a bit experienced, have the time and can afford the initial negative cashflow, then a good return can be had if the property is very cheap. As a rule of thumb, I'm interested in properties such as these if they can provide a return of 24 per cent or greater. Here you are paying less than £20,000 for a rental value of £400 per month. Always remember to double all initial budgeted refurbishment costs as experience shows that unforeseen problems emerge.

What to look for when viewing a property

Do not believe the myth that a property is only worth buying if you could see yourself living there. The fact is that you aren't going to live there, so what is the point of asking yourself if you could live there? You should ask, 'Would someone live here?' In a high-demand area people will live in a house as long as it has running hot water. I'm sure you've heard the horror stories from people living in London. I knew of 16 Australian and New Zealand backpackers sharing one room! I wouldn't live there, but the landlord found 16 people who would! You have to assess the demand.

The best way to assess the demand is to put a rogue advert in the local press. Place an ad before you own any property in that area for a property at market value rent. See how many calls you get. If you get one or two calls, then forget it. However, if you get 40+

calls then you know you've hit a hotspot. I have a few properties in Harlow, Essex and I placed an ad for one of my properties at slightly above market value and I had at least 40 calls and the property was let within two hours of the paper coming out.

When viewing a property check for:

Kitchen	Is the kitchen big enough to accommodate a small dining table? This is attractive if there is only one reception room and it turns the kitchen into a kitchen-diner.
Smallest bedroom	If the smallest bedroom is smaller than 6' 6" in any direction then it is not a bedroom! You need to be able to get a bed in a bedroom, hence this room can only be considered as a study or a baby's room. You need to consider this when considering what type of tenant you are looking for. If you are looking for two professional people to share a two-bedroom flat, then the second bedroom must be bigger than 6' 6".
Bathroom	Is there a fitted shower? A bathroom is a lot more desirable if there is a power shower. If there are two bathrooms then the property is very desirable, even if it is only a shower room.
Heating	Is the heating system old? This can be costly to replace. If possible, get it checked prior to purchase. It is your legal duty to provide heating and to issue a gas safety record.

Electrics	Are the electric sockets old? This will tell you that at some point the whole electric system will need rewiring.
Service charges	If it is a flat, you will have to pay service charges. Ask the agent if he has any details of the service charges. Some places have exorbitant service charges that render the whole investment unprofitable. Avoid listed buildings as they have frequent redecoration policies that can be expensive.

If the property is in a reasonable condition, then buy it. If demand is good there should be no problem letting it out as long as the property is in reasonable condition.

Making an offer

If you suspect that there will be a lot of interest in the property because it is cheap, do not be afraid to simply offer the asking price. This way there is no to-ing and fro-ing, the deal is done on the day and the property is removed from the market. If the agent gets the asking price, there is no need for them to show the property to someone else.

If you've arranged your mortgage, give a copy of the acceptance letter from the lender to the estate agent. This will convince him that you can act quickly, you are serious about buying the property and you are not just someone off the street who has just seen this property and thinks they can make some money out of it without giving it much thought. If you can show

him your bank statement as well which proves you have the deposit, then do so. Anything that will convince the estate agent that you are serious will make him unlikely to show the property to someone else.

If you suspect that demand is not high for the property, but it is still a sound investment, then ask the agent how long it has been on the market. If it's been a while then go in low. I would say 75-80 per cent of the asking price. Ask the estate agent, 'Has it ever had an offer? What offers have been refused?' Then you will be able to gauge your entry offer. This is assuming you believe the agent! If you have built up a relationship with an agent this should not be an issue, but always be aware.

Always remember the rule of 12 when negotiating. Do not get carried away with the negotiations and put in an offer that breaks the rule of 12.

When the offer is accepted, they will almost certainly ask you for your solicitor's details. Have your solicitor arranged prior to placing an offer. Simply inform a solicitor that you will be using them for a future purchase. The agent will then write to your solicitor to confirm the sale and the solicitor will instruct you what to do from then on.

You have to be patient when buying properties. Under normal circumstances the purchase should take no longer than eight weeks from the date your offer was accepted. There are many things that can go wrong with a purchase and sometimes there is nothing you can do about it but sit back and wait. I have listed some of the things that can go wrong and what, if possible, you can do about it:

What can go wrong	What to do about it	What can go wrong	What to do about it
Vendor withdraws property from market.	If the vendor has decided to keep the property there is nothing you can do about it. If he has decided to sell to someone else, then find out the selling price and go in even higher. If the property is worth more, then pay it! Remember, don't forget the rule of 12.	at the last minute, but you do not have the documentation or it will take a long time to get it.	then want further documentation, they should have asked for it earlier. Threaten to complain to the Financial Services Authority (FSA). If all else fails, try to get a compromise, i.e. if they want your mortgage statement to prove you have kept up to date on your mortgage payments in the last 12 months, offer them your bank statements for the last 12 months.
Survey fails or surveyor undervalues property.	Find out what it failed on. Ask the the vendor to remedy the problems. Do not, under any circumstances, offer to contribute to the cost of any remedial work. This is because after he has remedied the problems he may not sell to you and you will find it difficult to get your money back. If the property has been undervalued, it is difficult to persuade the valuer to value it up, but it is worth a try. Consider approaching another lender for revaluation or contributing the difference in the purchase price and the valuation.	The flow of documentation between solicitors is slow or nonexistent.	Ring your estate agent and get them to chase for you. The agent's wages depend on the sale of the property so he will have an interest in the sale occurring sooner rather than later. Ring your solicitor and ask what the hold-up is. Ask your solicitor if there is anything you can do. If you really want the property, you have to be prepared to do some of the acquisition work yourself. If it is proving impossible to get certain documentation from the freeholders when buying the leasehold, then consider losing the property.
The mortgage company require further documentation	Kick up a fuss! If they've approved your mortgage but		

What can go wrong	What to do about it
	This is because when it comes to selling the property you will probably have the same problems and purchasers will get fed up and pull out.

If things are progressing normally, however, then let your solicitor do everything, as this is what you are paying him for. Only react when your solicitor has informed you of a problem or you haven't heard anything for six weeks.

It's advisable, prior to exchange of contracts, that you view the property to see that it is still in the state you first viewed it as exchanged contracts are legally binding. If kitchen appliances were included in the sale, then check that they still remain there. Check that the carpets and curtains remain and the condition of the property has not deteriorated.

Once the purchase is complete, you then have the task of finding the right tenant…

Buying at auction

I have never bought a property at auction. The main reason being that you have to be able to proceed quickly. This means that the property has to be paid in full within 21-28 days, otherwise you lose your deposit which could be as much as 25 per cent of the purchase price. If you are getting a mortgage on the property then the lender has to be able to act quickly as well. Unfortunately, I do not have much faith in lenders to act quickly enough to ensure that payment is received in time.

There are definitely bargains to be had. If you have the nerves to buy at auction then I recommend you follow these 10 steps created by Giulia De Marco from Gold solicitors:

Step 1 – Go to an auction!

Most property auctions are open to the public. If you are interested, the best preparation starts with going along and getting a feel for what happens. It will also help to get rid of any unfounded fears; for example, you will not end up having to buy a property just because you nodded your head at the wrong time!

Step 2 – Register

Register with all the known auctioneers in the UK. They will put you on their mailing list and send you their auction catalogues. Catalogues usually give you a guide price for each property. It is important to note that this is not a valuation of the property; it is only an estimate of what the auctioneers or their clients expect the property to fetch at auction. There is no guarantee that the property will fetch that price and often it can go for considerably more than the guide price (and, it can go for less). It should also not be considered as a basis for the valuation which a surveyor might give the property.

Step 3 – Get the sales schedule and view

Once you have your catalogue, you may see some properties of interest. Telephone the auctioneers and see if they have any more details on the property or a sales schedule. They will also tell you the arrangements for viewing the property.

Go and visit the property if this is possible. In viewing a property you need to familiarise yourself with the area. If you do not know the area it is a good idea to view the property during the day and then at night-time. What seems a quiet street during the day may turn into the house from hell if a pub discharges its regulars at 11 o'clock on your doorstep! A chat with the neighbours or local police can reveal what kind of neighbourhood it is. Ask yourself what are your requirements. If you have children, you may wish to check out the local school. These are merely suggestions; the decoration of a house is not the only thing you should be checking when viewing or considering purchasing. This is not an exhaustive list of all the checks you should carry out before buying the property.

Step 4 – Instruct your solicitor

If you have viewed the property and wish to proceed, it is very important that you contact your solicitor as soon as possible. The sooner you instruct your solicitor, the sooner he can advise you on all matters. If you instruct your solicitor on the day of the auction or after successfully bidding, the solicitor is limited on what advice and action he can give you. Leave plenty of time

for your solicitor to be able to provide you with the fullest assistance and advice.

The purchase of a property at an auction is entirely different from purchasing a property being privately marketed. For example, if you are successful in your bid at the auction you are immediately committed to proceeding or face the possibility of being sued for breach of contract. Another example is that the contract to purchase the property at auction may specify that you take the title as it exists. This and the other conditions that apply depend on what the legal package is for that particular property. Your solicitor would wish therefore to examine the title deeds and legal package and provide you with a full report prior to you bidding at the auction. You or your solicitor may also wish to make enquiries of the local authority and carry out other searches all before the date of the auction. The moral of this is that the early bird catches the worm (and all the best bird houses!).

Step 5 – Financing

If you are going to bid for a property at an auction then you will be committing yourself on the day. It is therefore important to ensure that you have all the necessary financing of this transaction in place.

If you are seeking to obtain a mortgage over the property, then the lender will require a survey of the property to be carried out. Even if you are purchasing the property by cash it is still recommended that you carry out a survey. It is important to know exactly what you are purchasing! What seemed a very competitive price at auction might not be if you discover you have to spend £10,000 on remedying timber defects which you had not budgeted for. If you are obtaining a mortgage, it is even more important that you contact your solicitor in good time. Your mortgage offer will have conditions attached and it is important that your solicitor can check that these conditions can be complied with. Remember, your solicitor will be able to assist in appointing a surveyor or interpreting the survey results.

Step 6 – Bidding

If after consultation with your solicitor and surveyor you decide to bid at the auction, there are a couple of important things to note.

Don't worry, swatting at that fly or developing a nervous tick will not result with you being the proud owner of a holiday cottage in Shetland when you were looking for a townhouse in Glasgow!

If you are successful on the day of auction then you will require to pay a deposit; this must be arranged prior to the auction. It is usually around 10 per cent, but can vary. It has to be in cleared funds that are cash or banker's draft. The auctioneer will advise what is acceptable.

If you are unable to attend the auction in person, it may be possible to bid by proxy or by telephone, but you must contact the auctioneers beforehand to arrange this.

It is important that you check on the day of the auction whether there have been any amendments which have been made that

would have an effect on the title of the property or the value of the property. If you are uncertain about the effect of any alterations, then contact your solicitor or surveyor for advice. Also check that the property has not been withdrawn from the auction or sold prior to the auction. Sometimes the seller will consider a pre-auction offer and it may be worthwhile investigating this option.

When you are bidding for the property, ensure that you do not get carried away by offering more than you can afford. Do your budgeting beforehand and stick to it. Remember, once you have signed up on the day you have entered into a contract. After you have completed your bid, you will be approached by one of the auctioneer's clerks and you will be asked to provide your details. This will include your name, address, telephone number, method of payment of the deposit and some proof of identification. A contract will then be prepared for your signature.

Step 7 – Successful bid

If your bid is successful, this is not the end; rather it is just the beginning. For instance, it may be a condition that you are required to insure the property straight away. Your solicitor will explain these and other conditions. The date of entry will normally be 28 days later, when the remainder of the purchase price is paid. This again will be stipulated in the contract.

Step 8 – Unsuccessful bid

If a property doesn't reach the reserve price at the auction, then the auctioneers may withdraw it. It is always worth leaving your details with the auctioneers afterwards as the seller may consider a lower price shortly after the auction.

Step 9 – From contract to settlement

Again, as soon as you have been successful, contact your solicitor who will complete the conveyancing. This will include that in exchange for payment of the full price you will obtain a title to the property. This title is a deed, which is registered in the Public Registers and is of importance in establishing all your rights to the property.

Step 10 – Doubts

If you are still in any doubts contact your solicitor. Best of luck!

A list of all auction houses can be found in the reference chapter.

Buying property at auction is covered in more depth in Lawpack's book *Buying Bargains at Property Auctions* by Howard Gooddie.

4 Finding the right tenant

It's no good just finding a tenant. It has to be the right tenant. What defines the right tenant will depend on the following factors:

1. The property
2. You!
3. Your lender

The property

If you have acquired a private one-bedroom riverside apartment in a central location, then a single mum on benefits is probably not the most suitable tenant. When looking at properties, it's a good idea to build up a picture of the tenant you think is most suited to it. A tenant can only fall into one of eight general categories based on the size of the family unit and whether he is working or claiming benefit. The table on page 28 suggests which property is suited to each category of tenant.

So, if you buy a private one-bedroom flat, you know that the right tenant is a working single person or couple. You need only advertise for that tenant – 'suit working person or couple', the advert might read. If you misplace a tenant at your property, it will only lead to the hassle of finding another tenant later on. It's worth noting that a two+-bedroom ex-local authority house meets six out of the eight tenant categories.

You could use this table to dictate the type of property you buy. For example, if there are a lot of single parent DSS claimants in the area looking for properties, then a two-bedroom ex-local authority flat might be the right property to go for. If you wish to go for the minimum risk route, then go for the two+-bedroom ex-local authority house.

You!

If you are going to manage the property yourself then the most important person in this whole tenant-choosing process is YOU! If you feel you can get on and deal with only a certain category of people, then choose them exclusively. If you're a professional person used to dealing with only professional people, then steer towards private properties in the nicer areas and vice versa.

Personally, I have no prejudices or hang ups – apart from two:

1. People who can't speak English.
2. Young couples under 25.

It can be very difficult to extract rent from tenants when you cannot communicate with them. If there is an initial language barrier, then I can only foresee problems. Unless there is an intermediary, such as a social services officer because social

	Claiming benefit	Working
Single person	Ex-local authority studio or one-bedroom flat. If you are running a rent-a-room scheme, then a room in an ex-local authority house.	Any – he may require just a room to lay his head or require a three-bedroom house because he wants a computer room and a spare room. If he can pay the rent, then he can dictate where he wants to live.
Single parent	Two-bedroom + ex-local authority flat. If you let a one-bedroom flat to them they will only be looking to move to somewhere bigger and you will have to find another tenant again.	Two-bedroom ex-local authority or private house is preferable, as it will have a garden.
Couple	Ex-local authority studio/one-bedroom flat only. DSS are unlikely to pay market rent for a two-bedroom flat for a couple when they can quite comfortably live in a studio/one-bedroom flat.	Any – for the same reasons as above.
Family	Two+-bedroom ex-local authority house. A family will invariably want a property with a garden.	Two+-bedroom ex-local authority or private house. A family will invariably want a property with a garden.

Table 4.1. The eight categories of tenant

services are paying the rent, then it's okay. Otherwise steer clear of such tenants.

Couples aged under 25 are always troublesome. The tenancy will only last as long as the relationship does. They think it's a great idea to move in together after knowing each other for only two months, but when the couple fall out, neither one takes responsibility for the rent. You're left with the task of chasing them both independently for the rent but when they blame each other, you're the loser. If a couple under 25 are the only ones interested in the property, ask them how long they have been together and if they have lived together before. Try to get a larger deposit – two months is ideal.

Your lender

If you are borrowing to finance the property purchase, then lenders often stipulate what type of tenant you can have. The main exclusions are DSS claimants and student lets. You need to check with your lender what exclusions they have and let this be the criteria for your selection of the lender.

Advertising for a tenant

There are five main ways of advertising for a tenant, the cheapest form of advertising first:

1. Contacting the local council (FREE)
2. Advertising with large local employers (FREE)
3. Contacting accommodation projects (FREE)
4. On the internet (possibly free)
5. Advertising in the local press
6. Through a letting agent

Contacting the local council

Councils have a waiting list of people looking for a place to live. Since councils have fewer council properties on their books, they are always pleased to hear from private landlords willing to let their properties to residents in the local area. The councils have lists of working and unemployed people as well as refugees and asylum seekers.

I would advise that you write a letter detailing the property you have to let to the housing section of the local council and follow it up with a phone call. Councils can be slow, so I would not rely on this as your only source of finding a tenant.

Advertising with large local employers

There are two large local employers in the Harlow area. I wrote to both of their human resources departments detailing that I had various properties for their employees. I get a call once every other month, so I would not rely on this as your only source of finding a tenant.

Contacting local accommodation projects

Local accommodation projects are always on the lookout for willing landlords to take on homeless people in the area. Homeless does not mean that they are currently living rough – they simply do not have a fixed place of accommodation. These projects usually collect the rent and guarantee the rent if the tenant fails to pay. They do not charge for their services, as they are charities or non-profit organisations.

A list of accommodation projects is included in the reference chapter at the back.

On the internet

There are numerous sites on the web for landlords and tenants alike. Examples of sites where you can place an advertisement for free are:

www.letsdirect.co.uk
www.loot.com
www.roomsforlet.co.uk

Advertising in the local press

This is probably the most effective way of advertising. It is best to advertise in a paper that is delivered free locally so that your advert reaches every resident in that area. There are certain key elements you need to put in your advert:

- **Area:** You must say where the property is. It is no good to assume that the reader will know the area where the property is when the newspaper is distributed in a number of local areas. This way you avoid unwanted calls.

- **Private:** If it is in a private area (i.e. not ex-local authority), that is a selling point.

- **Furnished:** Again, if it is furnished, say so.

- **Number of bedrooms:** You must put the number of bedrooms the property has as readers will then know if your property can accommodate them.

- **Price:** In any advert, you must put the price. I always quote my properties as weekly rent e.g. £80 per week. This way the tenant assumes that the rent is £320 per month (as the tenant thinks there are four weeks in a month when there are actually 4.33 weeks in a month), when in fact it is £346 per calendar month. Your property will appear cheaper than other properties that are quoted per calendar month. If you price your property at £79 rather than £80 the impact is even more significant.

  However, do be aware not to include anything deliberately misleading as you will be in breach of the Property Midescriptions Act 1991.

- **Features:** If it's got a new bathroom, then say so! Anything that is not standard with a property such as a garage, separate dining room, large garden or new carpets will attract more interest.

- **Telephone number:** Do not only give out your mobile number! You will receive fewer calls as everyone knows that a five-minute call to a mobile costs a small fortune, especially to the people that you are trying to target. Put a landline down as well as a mobile. I have a freephone number which costs me 4p per minute to receive; a small price to pay to get someone talking about your property. Freephone providers are detailed in the reference chapter.

To find out about the local newspaper in the area of the property you have bought or thinking about buying, visit www.newspapersoc.org.uk.

Through a letting agent

This is the most expensive way to find a tenant. They usually charge one month's rent + VAT. But they will show prospective tenants round, run credit checks, ask for references, arrange a standing order and do an inventory check on the property. I would recommend this if you work or live far away from the property.

If you can't let the property

If you are having trouble letting the property, there is a number of things you can do. I suggest you do this, in the following order:

Action	Why?
Reduce the rent.	If you can't let it out at the price you want, then reduce the rent. It's the basic economics of supply and demand. I

Action	Why?
	suggest reducing the rent by £2 per week increments.
Widen the criteria for the type of tenant wanted.	If you've asked for non-smokers then consider smokers. The smell can be eradicated quite easily by a local cleaning company if need be.
Accept a tenant without a deposit.	A letting agent would be horrified by this advice. However, I have done this on a number of occasions, especially for DSS claimants who simply do not have that kind of cash to pay. I recommend this approach for properties that are not in the best of condition, and where the tenant is a family and are currently on benefits so the claim will go through smoothly. You have to ask yourself whether the tenant can do any more damage to the property considering its current state. Most people are looking for a place they can call home rather than moving into somewhere with the intention of wrecking it three months down the line.
Furnish the property.	This will be expensive and is no guarantee that

Action	Why?
	the place will attract tenants. Consider this if you are getting calls rejecting the property because it is unfurnished.
Sell it!	This is a drastic measure as I think any property in the UK is lettable – it's simply the rent you are asking for that will deter possible tenants. However, if you are experiencing trouble letting it, get out! Sell it and buy something else.

Credit-checking your tenants

You can check the credit of your tenant like a lender credit-checks a borrower. This costs between £17.50-£94.00, depending on what service you require. Some credit-checking agencies guarantee the rent if your tenant defaults. All letting agents insist that landlords do this, but I disagree. Credit checks are advisable for only certain types of tenants and areas. Let me explain by way of a table detailing the different type of tenant (private or DSS) and area (low and high demand for rental properties). A 'Yes' in the box means you should credit-check your tenant.

		Tenant	
		Private	Benefit claimant
Area	High demand for rental property	Yes	No
	Low demand for rental property	No	No

So only in one out of four circumstances would you normally obtain a credit check on your prospective tenant. The justification for this is as follows:

- **Private tenant in high demand area:** As the tenant is paying all the rent and you can afford to be choosy as there is high demand for your property, then it is worth credit- checking. This ensures that you get the best tenant. I would strongly advise you to get an employer's reference as confirmation that the company employs him and to use the credit check as only a supporting tool.

- **Private tenant in low demand:** If you have had few calls for your property and you wish to only have a private tenant, then you cannot be choosy. Most people will fail a credit check – even I do. I am a chartered accountant, but I have a default that I am currently investigating from 18 months ago for £4.89, which renders my credit check as a failure. So a credit check does not always guarantee the best tenant; it can only support the tenant's case. That's why it's important to get an employer's reference.

- **DSS tenant in high demand:** The council pays the majority of the rent, so there is no point credit-checking a tenant for,

say, a £10-a-week top-up. The tenant would probably fail the check anyway.

- **DSS tenant in low demand:** The same reason as above.

Credit-checking is also dependent on your risk factor. If you are a risk adverse investor (risk factor 1) then it is probably advisable to get the full credit check that guarantees the rent, if the tenant fails. If you are willing to accept some degree of risk (risk factor 2-6), then it is advisable to get a credit check in the circumstances noted above. If you are a risk taker (risk factor 7) like me, then never get a credit check. Get an employer's reference.

I use my common sense and intuition; it hasn't failed me yet. A prospective tenant who fails a credit check could be better than a tenant who passes a credit check. Let me explain. The two most common causes for someone to fail a credit check, even though their credit rating is still good, are:

1. **They've never had credit:** Just because someone has never had credit does not make them uncreditworthy. For example, you may have a university graduate looking to move into your property as he has just got his first job in the area. He may be from a good family who will bail him out if he gets into any money problems. One would imagine that he is responsible enough to take the financial commitment of a tenancy, considering he has gone to university. He will probably be earning in excess of the national average wage and will be able to afford the rent comfortably. Taking these factors on board, he may still fail a credit check. However, he may be the most suitable

tenant for your property after taking everything into consideration.

2. **Low value defaults:** I have a default for £4.89 as mentioned above. I would fail some credit checks because of this. A £4.89 default does not make me uncreditworthy under any circumstances. You have to look at the tenant's situation as a whole, rather than whether he passes or fails a credit check. Do not be afraid to ask what he earns and compare that to the rent you are charging. If the monthly rent is approximately one-third of their monthly income, then he can probably afford it.

The most common causes for a tenant to pass a credit check but ultimately end up defaulting are:

1. **He loses his job:** No amount of credit-checking can predict this.

2. **The tenant household splits up:** When couples split up, their financial commitments are the last to get a look-in. If you've let to a group of students and one of them leaves, it can then be very difficult to chase him or to get the rest of the household to make up the difference. Just because a tenant passes a credit check now, does not mean that they will honour their commitments in the future. Their circumstances have now changed – this is why people default!

3. **The tenant misbudgeted:** If this is the first time the tenant has ever taken on the responsibility of occupying and paying for a home, then it is possible that the tenant has miscalculated or omitted some of the other costs associated with running a home. Add in rates, council tax, electricity, etc., and the tenant quickly falls in arrears. Ask the tenant if they have ever run their own household and ascertain if the tenant is aware of all the costs involved in doing so.

So you can see that credit checks have limited use. The key questions you need to be asking yourself about the prospective tenant is:

- Can he afford it now and in the future?

- Has he got a temporary or permanent job?

- Has he got a supportive family and can you get them to be guarantors for the rent?

- Does he appear to know all the costs involved in running a household?

I assume that if someone can afford to pay more than a month's deposit and one week's rent in advance then he will probably be able to pay the rent in the future. So far I have not been very wrong; the times I have been wrong is when I have not taken a deposit and let a tenant move in with just one week's rent in advance. The tenant quickly falls into arrears because they cannot budget. That is why they never had a deposit in the first place!

Dealing with councils for housing benefit payments (DSS)

If you decide to accept someone on benefits, then the local council will pay most of the rent. Many investors do not like DSS tenants, but I have had little trouble with this type of tenant and once set up, the rent simply arrives at your doorstep. There is a number of key factors when dealing with the DSS:

- **You will get paid four weeks in arrears:** All councils pay four weeks in arrears. If cashflow is crucial, then do not take on DSS. Invariably the council initially will take anywhere between four weeks and 16 weeks to get paid. This is because you depend on the tenant providing all the information that the council requires. To help speed up the process, ensure that the application goes in long before the tenant moves into the property. Also, make sure that the original tenancy agreement and other original documents are sent to the Housing Benefit office promptly. Tenants should be asked to sign a letter of authority authorising the Housing Benefit office to provide information to the landlord. If the tenant is slow to respond to the council, consider issuing notices of eviction to the tenant to hurry him up.

- **Ensure that the benefit cheques get paid direct to you:** All housing benefit can be paid directly to the landlord if the tenant signs a consent form. It is a must if you take on DSS. This way you get paid directly by the council and avoid the tenants pocketing the cash.

- **Claw-backs:** If the rent from the Housing Benefit office is paid directly to you, you can present yourself with a potential problem that if the Housing Benefit office discovers that an overpayment of benefit has been made to a previous landlord of the tenant, it can deduct the overpayment from rent paid to you. To protect yourself, check out your tenants carefully and if possible, obtain a reference from the previous landlord. However, under new regulations which came into effect in October 2001, if you report (in writing) your suspicion of your tenant being fraudulent, the local authority will not claw-back from you, provided you have not colluded with the tenant in obtaining the overpayment.

The relationship between landlord and tenant

Your tenant is not your friend! If your friend approaches you wishing to live in one of your properties, then say no – make some excuse. We all know the feeling when we've lent a friend £20 on a night out and we then have to ask for the money back; we all hate doing it. There is a good reason why we don't like doing so and that is because money and friends don't mix. Many friends in the past have fallen out over very small amounts of money, let alone a month's rent.

If your tenant tries to become friendly with you, by inviting you to their Christmas party for instance, always decline. The relationship between landlord and tenant is strictly a business relationship and if this becomes blurred, then you are heading for trouble. This does not mean you have to be overly distant. Remember that you are in business with each other and that is the only reason why you know each other. For the relationship to last, the following simple contract needs to hold – you are supplying a safe property for the tenant to live in and the tenant is paying you the rent on time. Do not complicate matters by drifting into a friendship/business relationship.

Rent collection

You can collect your rent in four main ways:

1. Using a letting agent
2. Via your bank
3. Through the post
4. Face-to-face

Apart from using a letting agent, the way to collect the rent should be dictated by the tenant. You need to make the way the tenant pays their rent as easy as possible and this will be determined by the tenant. Your choice of tenant should not be dictated by the ease of collection of rent. The choice of tenant should be dictated by the factors mentioned above. It is your duty to work around the tenant if you want the right tenant and to receive the rent on time.

1. Using a letting agent

Letting agents can handle the whole process of letting your property. This involves finding a tenant, taking inventories, collecting or guaranteeing rent and dealing with all tenant and property problems –

sounds too good to be true. However, letting agents are expensive! For a full management service the fee charged can range from 12 per cent to 20 per cent + VAT of the rent collected. We accountants call this 'top line commission'. It is called this because they are charging commission on the rental income rather than the overall profit you are making. The expression 'top line' comes from the fact that income is the top line in any profit or loss account.

An agent's fee can wipe out a significant proportion of the profit you potentially could make. Look at this following example, where method 1 is with an agent and method 2 is without an agent:

	£	
	Method 1	Method 2
Rental income	400	400
Mortgage	(200)	(200)
Building insurance	(10)	(10)
Sundry expenses	(10)	(10)
Agent's fee (15% + VAT)	(70)	Nil
Net profit	110	180

We can see that a 15 per cent agent's fee can reduce your net profit by 40 per cent – basically just under halving the profit you would make if you did not have an agent! That is not to say you should not use an agent. You need to decide how involved you wish to be in the day-to-day running of the property you have just bought. I would use an agent in the following circumstances:

1. **You work full-time:** This is not to say that you shouldn't try without the help of an agent. I have a few properties that I have never seen since I first let them or I haven't spoken to the tenant since I first met them. This is because the

tenant's rent is paid directly into my bank account by standing order, nothing has gone wrong with the flat since I bought it and I get workmen to do the annual inspections. In this situation, who needs an agent? Only use an agent once letting your property has eaten into your leisure time or you've just simply got fed up. You do not want your tenant ringing you up complaining of a blocked drain when you are in the middle of an important meeting!

2. **The property is far away:** If a property is more than three hours' travel away, then it is probably better to use an agent. The gross yield must be very good, though; I would say 24 per cent is the minimum, if not higher. This is because you are using an agent and if you were only receiving a 12 per cent yield, after agent fees, you would be making a loss.

When I first started I used an agent, as I worked full-time and did not want to get bothered at work when something went wrong. Sometimes it can be very time-consuming chasing your tenant for rent. Remember letting agents are experts in handling tenants and cannot do only what you do, but they can do it better; that's their business!

The only time I use an agent now is for my properties in Norton, Middlesborough, which is at least four hours away from me by car. The rental yield on these properties is around 70 per cent! I can afford to use an agent when the profit margin is so high.

I would advise you to use an Association of Residential Letting Agents (ARLA)-accredited agent, as you are then insured against frauds committed by the agent and bankruptcy of the agent. This means that you would receive all the rents collected by the agent even if the rents were not handed over by the agent. Proof of the fraud would not be needed as the rents are covered by an insurance scheme backed by ARLA. ARLA agents can be found by visiting www.arla.co.uk.

2. Via your bank

Assuming your tenant has a bank account, you can set up a standing order that deposits the rent directly to your bank account from the tenant's bank account. I suggest you use the template on page 37 and ensure that it is sent to the tenant's bank branch at the time of the tenant signing the lease. This template will set up the standing order.

Another way you can collect rent through your bank is to ask the tenant to give you a series of post-dated cheques to cover the rent. So, for example, if he is to pay a rent of £400 on the first day of the month, then ask for six cheques for £400 dated the first of the month for the next six months. You then simply present these cheques when the cheques' dates become valid.

You could also give your tenant a paying-in book for your bank account. This is best for tenants who earn cash but do not have a bank account. This way the tenant could visit your branch and deposit the rent when possible, rather than you both organising a rendezvous for the tenant to hand over the cash.

STANDING ORDER SET-UP

PAYER:

Name:	*Put the tenant's full name here*
Branch:	*Put the tenant's bank branch and full address*
A/C number:	*Put the tenant's account number here*
Sort code:	*Put the tenant's bank branch's sort code here*

PAYEE:

Name:	*Put your full name here*
Branch:	*Put your bank branch's name and full address*
A/C number:	*Put your account number here*
Sort code:	*Put your bank branch's sort code here*

PAYMENT DETAILS:

Amount:	*Put the weekly or monthly rent here*
Transfer date:	*Put the first date you want the transfer to occur here*
Repeat:	*Put the frequency either weekly or monthly here*
Last transfer date:	*Always put 'To be notified in writing'*

Please could you set up the above standing order on my behalf as soon as possible, to ensure that the first transfer payment is paid on time.

_____   _____
Date   Signed (the tenant)

_____
Print Name

Please now send on to the payer's bank branch.

Fig 4.1. Standing order set-up

3. Through the post

I receive the majority of my rent through the post. This is either from the tenant themselves or from the council housing benefit departments. I prefer this method as it is easier to keep a mental check of who is supposed to be paying (because a cheque physically lands at your door on a regular basis), rather than continually checking your bank account.

I have one tenant who consistently sends me the rent cheque by recorded delivery. As I am never up when the postman knocks on my door (around 8am), I have to go to the sorting office to get my cheque. I asked my tenant not to send it by recorded delivery but he prefers to do it that way, so I have to accept that I have to go to the sorting office every week! Remember, the tenant always dictates the method of payment.

Under no circumstances should you allow the tenant to pay cash through the post.

4. Face-to-face

It is unlikely that the tenant will insist on face-to-face collection of the rent. You may feel more comfortable collecting the rent face-to-face so you can see what state the property is being kept in. If the tenant is happy with you collecting the rent that way, it is important that you do not let him feel that you are checking up on him. This will make him feel uncomfortable and could lead to him moving out. If you have chosen the tenant right, you will not need to check up on him so often and you can revert to the payment method that suits the tenant.

Minimising void periods

There are five key ways to minimise the time between the old tenant leaving and the new tenant entering:

1. Neutral decoration
2. Invest in high demand areas
3. Be less fussy!
4. Invest in a property for which there is high demand
5. Advertise the property in adequate time

Neutral decoration

This is simply common sense. If the property has been decorated in a feminine way, such as flowery borders and pink colours, then you are already cutting out half the market: the boys! If the property has been decorated to a specific taste, such as chintz, then you are going to exclude tenants that don't like chintz.

You have to make your property suitable for the widest range of tenants. Ensure that the decoration is neutral and not personalised. Tenants personalise their properties with their possessions. You have to rely on luck, if you do not neutralise the decoration, that the right tenant turns up when the property becomes available to rent again.

Invest in high demand areas

My philosophy is that any property can be let out eventually. If you want to minimise the time the property is left vacant between tenants, then go for a property where you know demand is high for rented properties. A local letting agent will be able to tell you this. Also you can speak to the accommodation projects listed in the reference chapter or you can place a rogue ad in the local paper and see how many calls you get.

Investing in high demand areas has a cost. It is probable that high demand areas will have higher property purchase prices than a low demand area. This will affect your yield but remember, do not break the rule of 12! You will also be competing against other landlords so you will have to be able to move on the purchase quickly; have your finance in place.

Be less fussy!

If you are excluding a certain type of tenant then you run the risk of having a void period. The more prospective tenants you exclude, the greater the likelihood of the property being vacant. If you are relying on your strict perception of the right tenant to appear around the time your existing tenant decides to leave, then you are relying heavily on luck.

Ways of becoming less fussy without compromising too much on the quality of tenant are:

- Consider non-professional tenants. There is nothing to say a professional is any better than a hard-working builder as a tenant, so do not advertise for 'professionals only'.

- Consider pets. You could consider cats but no dogs, or accept only caged pets. What damage could a goldfish do?

- Consider DSS. I have no problem with DSS claimants. You could just consider claimants on incapacity benefit rather than job seekers' allowance.

Invest in a property for which there is high demand

As mentioned elsewhere, a two-bed ex-local authority property generally covers a high percentage of prospective tenants. If there is high demand for a certain type of property, then invest in that type of property. Currently there is high demand for private two-bed flats in London because there is less stigma now for professionals to share. Again, there will be high demand for these properties from investors and private people and this will drive the purchase price up, consequently affecting your yield.

Advertise the property in adequate time

Your existing tenant has to give you sufficient notice if he wishes to vacate the property, usually of one month. This gives you ample time to find a tenant. If you've had a good relationship with your tenant, your tenant will probably not mind showing prospective tenants around during his one-month notice period.

As soon as you do get notice, then follow the instructions given in this chapter for advertising for a tenant. There is no point in hanging around, as the longer you leave it the less time you have to find one.

However, do remember that by law a landlord must not sign a new tenancy agreement until the existing tenant has moved out. Otherwise, you will be in breach of contract.

5 Expanding your portfolio

Okay, so I've told you how to get one property. But how do you get 50 properties in five years? The key is remortgaging. Remortgaging is all about releasing the equity that's locked up in the property that you currently own.

So if you've bought your first property for £50,000 and you can get it revalued in excess of £70,000, then you can access some of that £20,000 equity to buy further properties. It is this release of equity that enables you to buy further properties, as this equity can be used as deposits for further properties.

The revaluation trick

I bought a property in June 2001 for £23,500 in Northampton with a £6,000 deposit, did nothing to it, got it revalued at £42,000 by a different lender four months later, released £18,000, used this for further deposits and bought four more properties! In effect, one property enabled me to get four further properties. This is possible if you watch out for these bargains.

The reason a £23,500 property can be revalued at £42,000 is that when you get a revaluation the valuer is only giving an opinion on what the property is worth and it is only a guide. However, the mortgage company takes this as the market value to lend against.

When filling out the form for a remortgage never be conservative about what you think the property is worth. If you bought it for £23,500 say it is worth double that, like I did (£47,000) and the valuer may come back at £42,000. This actually happened. This way you can raise the maximum amount of the cheapest borrowings to buy further properties.

I know the effective mortgage payment increases when you remortgage, but the additional properties you buy and the income these further generate more than compensate for the increased mortgage payment. Let me show you by way of example:

Rob buys his first property two years ago for £60,000 with a 25 per cent deposit.

Property 1

Rental	£600
Mortgage (at 6%)	£225
Profit	£375
Valuation	£60,000
Borrowings	£45,000

If an application is made that revalues the property at £80,000 and the lender is willing to lend 85 per cent then the funds that can be raised are:

£80,000 x 85 per cent - £45,000 = £27,250.

With this £27,250, Rob can buy three further properties for £60,000 each placing £9,000 deposit each (3 x £9,000 = £27,000) but the original mortgage payment has gone up on property 1 due to the extra borrowings:

Property	1	2	3	4	Total
Rental £	600	600	600	600	2,400
Mortgage £ (6%)	361	255	255	255	1,126
Profit £	*239*	*345*	*345*	*345*	*1,274*

So, by a combination of revaluing, releasing equity due to increased borrowings and purchase of further investment properties, profit nearly trebles from £375 to £1,274. This is because the equity Rob has released, borrowed at six per cent, generates income far in excess of six per cent due to the purchase of three investment properties. The profit generated from these three further properties covers the additional interest cost of remortgaging the original property and an extra £899!

Do not be worried if the revaluation breaks the rule of 12, i.e. the property gets revalued to £80,000 but you are only getting £600 per month rental. Remember borrowing is cheap, so if you can get borrowings at six per cent to get a return in excess of 20 per cent on property, then do it. Only hesitate from doing this when borrowing rates are in excess of returns that can be had from the property.

Risk analysis for the future

This section deals with things that can go wrong. When you are in business you are always susceptible to going bust. It happened to Railtrack, so it can happen to you! What makes a successful business is not only the ability to make a profit and generate cash but to continue to do so. This means being able to:

1. react to changing market conditions quickly;

2. protect against threats to your long-term income.

React to changing market conditions quickly

The profit you generate is dependent on two basic elements: rental income and mortgage expenditure. If either of these elements changes in your favour (market rental income increases or market mortgage expenditure decreases), then you are stupid not to capitalise on this. You need to keep your eye on the market for both these elements. The easiest way to do this is:

- **Rental income:** Simply scan the 'accommodation to let' adverts in the local paper once every two months or so and see what a similar property to the one you own is going for. If the market value rent has risen for your property, then increase your rent accordingly when you are able to do so. You are able to do this after the duration of the lease has expired.

- **Mortgage expenditure:** If you're on a fixed rate and interest rates are dropping, then consider remortgaging at a lower rate. Approach your lender initially and tell them that you are considering remortgaging and they may even reduce the rate – it's worth a try.

The more money you make by keeping abreast of changing market conditions, the more you have set aside for further reinvestment, hence further profit.

Protect against threats to your long-term income

The key to managing risk in the long-term is diversification – 'not putting all your eggs in one basket'. The way to do this is to vary the following factors when investing in property:

- **Area:** Try to invest in different towns and cities. Rental demand or property price changes can vary according to area due to significant increases in crime rates, redundancies, pollution, etc.

- **Property:** Buy both private and ex-local authority properties. Consider both flats and houses. Do not stick exclusively to two-bedroom properties; consider studios and four-bedroom properties. This way you are not stuck with seeking a particular type of tenant.

- **Tenant:** Consider both DSS and private tenants.

- **Borrowings:** Go for a mixture of fixed and variable borrowings. Do not stick exclusively with one lender.

The following table on page 44 details the threats to your long-term income and how diversification minimises the impact of the threat. This is not an exhaustive list. These are just some of the threats that I have faced but have been able to weather due to diversification.

Threat	Effect of diversification
Interest rates increase dramatically.	Because some of your borrowings are fixed, the increase in interest rates will not fully impact on your mortgage cost. How risk averse you are will depend on the ratio of fixed to variable borrowings. Even if you are of risk factor 7, I still recommend you fix some of your borrowings cost.
Demand for rental properties in the area fall significantly.	This could be due to heavy job losses in the area. As you have properties in other areas, the impact of the job losses is not felt on the whole portfolio. If this does happen, the key is to cover just your mortgage payment until demand picks up. If you drop your rent to an attractive price just above your mortgage payment, you will ensure that you will get a tenant before most other landlords. If it is unlikely that demand will pick up, then consider selling.
Changes in housing benefit entitlement.	Some councils have cut back on housing benefit and insist that the tenant contributes more to the rent. The tenant usually struggles to do this. If you have invested in different areas, your portfolio is not subject to one council change. Also, if you have taken on a combination of private and DSS tenants then the impact is lessened.

Table 5.1. Threats & effects of diversification

6 Tax

We all hate paying tax, but we cannot ignore it. This chapter deals with the key figures when calculating your tax and how to legally minimise your tax bill. Let's identify the types of tax you will be subject to if you invest in property.

Types of tax

There are two types of tax that property is subject to:

1. **Income tax:** This tax is applied to the profit generated from the renting out of the property. It has to be paid every year in half-yearly instalments on 31st January and 31st July. Taxable profit is deemed to be taxable rental income minus allowable expenditure.

   Taxable rental income, and more importantly, allowable expenditure will be defined in detail in this chapter so you can easily calculate and reduce your taxable profit by claiming all allowable expenditure.

2. **Capital Gains Tax:** This tax is only applied once the property has been sold. It is essentially the tax applied to the profit you have made from selling the property.

   Detailed below are certain reliefs that you can claim to minimise your Capital Gains Tax bill to zero!

Income Tax

You will only ever pay tax on your taxable profits, that is to say you have to make money before you pay tax. Income has to exceed expenditure; if you have not achieved this, you should not even be interested in this chapter. If you are in the position where income does exceed expenditure, then read on.

The equation

The simple equation for calculating your income tax bill is:

Taxable rental income - allowable expenditure = taxable profit

So in order for your taxable profit to be the lowest possible, then the 'taxable rental income' must be minimised and the 'allowable expenditure' must be maximised.

Minimising 'taxable rental income'

This is very difficult to do. Taxable rental income is deemed to be any rental income earned in the period, the period usually being the tax year 6th April to 5th April. 'Earned' means not only what the tenant has paid but also what the tenant owes even if it has not yet been paid. Basically, there are no tricks in reducing taxable rental income, apart from one: if a tenant is 14 days in arrears, you can consider that debt as a bad debt and not include it as taxable rental income. If the tenant does end up paying, you can include the income in the following accounting period. Fourteen days outstanding rent is in real terms not that much and you'll have to pay tax on the income in the following year anyway. The only real benefit is cashflow. This is because you save slightly on your tax bill and defer payment on this omitted rental income until your next tax return the following year.

Maximising 'allowable expenditure'

This is easier to do than minimising rental income. This is because the Inland Revenue grants certain allowances based on certain definitions, as well as allowable expenditure. This means expenditure and allowances can be deducted from the taxable rental income to derive the taxable profit. The two pure definitions that you need to remember for allowable expenditure and taxable allowances, as stated by the Inland Revenue, are:

1. 'Any costs you incur for the sole purposes of earning business profits'

2. 'Capital allowances on the cost of buying a capital asset, or a wear-and-tear allowance for furnished lettings'

1. 'Any costs you incur for the sole purposes of earning business profits'

Any expense you incur 'wholly, necessarily and exclusively' for the business is fully deductible from your rental income. Any personal expenditure that you make that relates to the business is partly tax deductible from your income. To make sure you include all expenses that are allowable against your rental income refer to the following checklists of expenses for inclusion in your Tax Return:

Fully tax deductible expenses:

Expense	Description
Repairs & maintenance	All repairs and maintenance costs are fully tax deductible. Where the property has been altered so extensively that it is deemed to be reconstructed the property is then considered to be 'modified' rather than 'repaired', hence no amount of the expense is allowed. The only amount allowed would be the estimated cost of maintenance or repair made unnecessary by the modification. Examples of repairs and maintenance expenditure that are fully tax deductible are: • Painting and decoration • Damp treatment • Roof repairs • Repairs to goods supplied with the property e.g. a washing machine
Finance charges	Any interest you pay on a loan that you took out to acquire a property is fully tax deductible. It is only the interest and not the capital repayment part that is tax deductible. If any of the finance raised (the loan) is used for personal use, such as a holiday, then the interest paid on the amount paid for the holiday is not tax deductible. The typical

Expense	Description
	interest payments that are allowed are:
	• Interest on the mortgage taken out to get the property • Interest on any secured or unsecured loans taken out to get the property
	Arrangement fees charged by a lender are also tax deductible.
	Interest paid on the car you use to run the property business is partly tax deductible – see below.
Legal & professional fees	Allowable expenditure is: • Letting agent's fees for the collection in rent, including the VAT (unless you are VAT-registered) • Legal fees for evicting tenants • Accountancy fees for preparing your accounts Disallowable expenditure is: • Surveyor fees initially paid out to value the property (unless the survey was unsuccessful and you never acquired the property, in which case it is a fully deductible expense) • Legal fees incurred through the purchase of the property When it comes to calculating the capital gain when you sell the property, these expenses are added to the purchase

Expense	Description
	price. The capital gain is calculated: Gain = selling price - purchase price This results in the purchase price being higher than the actual price paid because of the addition of initial professional fees. So the taxable gain is lower. These fees are subject to full indexation, as is the purchase price, to allow for price inflation – see 'Capital Gains Tax' below. So you do get some tax relief but only further down the line, when you sell the property.
Council Tax, electricity, water & gas	If you are renting out all the rooms, all the usual running costs involved with a property are fully tax deductible. This assumes that none of the tenants make a contribution to the bills. If you let out your property inclusive of all the bills, then you can fully charge all the bills you include with the rent. If you let out your property exclusive of all bills (which is the usual way), then you cannot claim. Remember, you can only claim the expense if you actually paid it!
Insurance	• Buildings insurance • Contents insurance • Rental guarantee Insurance premiums are fully tax deductible. Life assurance

Expense	Description
	premiums are not, as this is personal expenditure. Car insurance is, but only partly – see below.
Advertising	Any advertising costs in connection with finding a tenant or selling your property are fully tax deductible. This includes: • Newspaper adverts • Agent's commission
Ground rent	This is the rent you pay if you own a leasehold flat, typically a nominal amount of £50 per annum.
Service charges	Service charges are incurred if you own a leasehold flat. If you pay these charges, then they are fully tax deductible.
Letting agent fees	Any fee that is charged by a letting agent is fully tax deductible, apart from any fees charged for leases created for longer than a year. If a fee is charged for creating a 5-year lease, only one fifth of the fee can be charged for each year.
Stationery	Any stationery costs incurred in connection with running your property business are fully tax deductible. This will include items such as: • All paper and envelopes • Postage • All printing expenditure

Partly tax deductible expenses:

Expense	Description
Motor expenses	Motor costs are allowable but only when your car is used in connection with the property business. It is up to you to decide how much time you think you spend using your car for private use and business use. It has to be reasonable. Once you have decided on the split of personal to business, say 70% personal, 30% business, you can charge the business percentage against your taxable rental income, in this case 30%. Typical motor expenses are: • Car insurance • Fuel • Servicing and repairs • Interest paid on the loan taken out to acquire the car A fraction of the purchase price of the car can also be taken into account as an allowance – see below. I charge 80% of my motor expenses to the business. This is because I have 50 properties to maintain around the country and I spend 80% of my driving time on business engagements.
Telephone calls	Again this is like motor expenses. If you spend 30% of your time on the phone in connection with your business, then charge 30% of:

Expense	Description
	• Total landline call charges • Total line rental for your landline • Total mobile call charges • Total line rental for your mobile If there are obvious large private calls (say in excess of £5), then exclude these from the total call expense when calculating the 30% charge. If you have a fax line, then charge 100% of fax expenses as it is easy to convince the Inland Revenue that you own a fax machine for business use!

Again, this is not an exhaustive list. To make sure you legally maximise your allowable taxable expenditure, you have to remember the following two principles:

- Include expenditure if it is 'wholly, necessarily and exclusively' needed for the business. If it is, include it. If it is not, exclude it or partly include it.

- Include a proportional amount of expenditure that is split between business and personal such as motor expenses and telephone calls.

2. 'Capital allowances on the cost of buying a capital asset, or a wear-and-tear allowance for furnished lettings'

This basically means that you can either charge:

- 25 per cent of the cost of any asset used to furnish the property, or
- 10 per cent of the rent

as a tax-deductible expense. You cannot do both. I would always recommend doing the latter, charging 10 per cent of the rent, because once you opt to do one or the other, you cannot change for the duration of your business. The reason I recommend 10 per cent of the rent is because 10 per cent of the rent is likely to be greater than 25 per cent of the cost of the asset. If this is not the case now, it will probably be in the future. It is better to suffer the lower deductible expense now for the benefit in the future.

You can still claim capital allowances for any asset that you use in the business, such as motor vehicles, but it will be restricted to the business element only. So in the example above of the motor vehicle with 30 per cent business use, a car used in the business costing £5,000 would attract the following relief:

30 per cent x 25 per cent x £5,000 = £375.

You can never charge the cost of an item that you intend to use for longer than one year against your rental income. Anything purchased for use longer than one year is deemed to be an asset and only 25 per cent of the cost can be charged each year.

Capital Gains Tax

This tax only arises when you sell the property. The capital gain is worked out as:

Sale price - purchase price - indexation allowance/taper relief = capital gain

The sale price is deemed to be the price achieved after deducting estate agent costs, solicitors' fees and any other expenses that were incurred wholly, necessarily and exclusively in the sale of the property.

The purchase price is the cost of the property, plus all survey and legal costs.

Indexation allowance and taper relief

Up until 5 April 1998, you were allowed to set against any capital gain the element of that profit which was caused by inflation. In other words, you didn't have to pay tax on inflationary gains. This amount, called indexation, was calculated by working out the amount the retail price of the house had increased between date of purchase and date of sale.

Since 6 April 1998, indexation has no longer been an allowable deduction. However, you can still claim it but it can only be calculated from the gain acquired before 5 April 1998.

The Government instead have now introduced taper relief, which came into effect on 5 April 1998. According to the number of completed years that the asset has been owned after that date, only a percentage of the gain will be chargeable. This relief is very complicated to calculate and as a result, I strongly advise you to take professional advice or see if the Inland Revenue can process your query quickly.

How to reduce your capital gain

If property investment is your main source of income and the property you have bought is deemed to be a business asset, any capital gain that you do achieve from the sale of your property can be offset against either one of the following three reliefs:

- **Rollover relief:** If you fully invest the whole proceeds from the sale in another business asset e.g. another investment property within two years or one year prior of the date of the disposal, then the capital gain does not attract Capital Gains Tax.

- **Retirement relief:** If you are over the age of 50 and retiring, or retiring due to ill health at any age, then the capital gain is exempt from tax. This is subject to certain limits.

- **Enterprise Investment Scheme (EIS) shares or Venture Capital Trusts (VCT) shares:** If you invest the proceeds of the sale of the property in EIS shares or VCT shares, there is no Capital Gains Tax to pay. This is a government incentive for investors to invest in company start-ups to encourage new business.

7 Legal aspects

The legal aspects a landlord faces can be split into three broad categories:

- Contractual
- Regulatory
- All-encompassing

This chapter provides an overview of the main legal issues that face a landlord. Further in-depth discussion on landlord and tenant law can be found in Lawpack's *Residential Lettings Guide*.

Contractual

Contractual refers to the legal contracts that you will sign and enter into. You will be bound to fulfil your obligations under the terms of the contract. Breach of terms can result in you being sued and ultimately paying damages to the aggrieved party. As a landlord you will enter into legal contracts with your:

1. Lender
2. Tenant
3. Insurer
4. Letting agent

Lender

Prior to entering into a contract with a lender, it has to know about you. The lender asks you a number of questions and expects the truth. If it is discovered that you have misled the lender by any of your answers to its questions, it can demand repayment of the loan in full plus all recovery costs. It can also inform the police and charge you with obtaining finance by deception. This is fraud and you can go to prison.

Once the lender has established that you are a person worth lending to, it insists you sign its contract. The lender sets the terms of the contract. As the lender has lent money to you, it is its right to set the terms of the contract. Unless you are borrowing a large sum of money then you can never include any clauses in the contract based on your terms; that's just the way it is. The key terms of the contract are:

- **Payment:** You have to pay the mortgage repayments on the dates the lender dictates. If you fail to do so, the lender can repossess the property.

- **Maintenance:** You must keep the property in a good state of repair, fit enough to be habitable.

- **Occupation:** You must not leave the property vacant for more than 30 days.

Tenant

There are several legal documents that are created when you find a suitable tenant:

1. An inventory and statement of condition
2. An Assured Shorthold Tenancy Agreement
3. An eviction order

1. An inventory and statement of condition

An inventory, sometimes called a statement of condition, is a document listing all items that are in the property, including their descriptions, quantities and condition. Both the tenant and the landlord should sign this list. When the tenant decides to leave the property you can check the list to see what is left in the property. If there are any deviations from the list you can charge the tenant to correct the deviation. So, for example, if there were four dining chairs when the tenant moved in and now there are only three, you can deduct the cost of replacing the dining chair from the tenant's deposit.

If you get an inventory done, it will ensure that the tenant thinks that you care about the place you are letting and he will be less likely to damage the property. If the condition of the carpet is recorded, the tenant is more likely to remove any stains caused, as he fears that you will deduct cleaning costs from his deposit.

The best format is to prepare the inventory on a room-to-room basis with columns for the item, condition and quality. Also, do allow space for alterations to the condition, signatures and date, plus a statement mentioning that the document is an accurate description of the property and will be used to check for any damages at the end of the tenancy.

Produce two copies – one for you and one for the tenant. It is advisable to go through the inventory with the tenant when he moves in and ensure that any alterations are made to both copies so that the documents are always identical.

To avoid any disputes, one can approach an independent company to prepare the inventory. You can find a professional inventory clerk near you from the website of the National Register of Inventory Clerks at www.nric.co.uk. Alternatively, one can be found in the Yellow Pages or by visiting www.yell.com.

2. An Assured Shorthold Tenancy (AST)

This is an agreement between the landlord and tenant defined by the Housing Act 1988 (which was slightly modified by the Housing Act 1996). It binds both parties to certain duties and obligations. The main features of a tenancy agreement are:

- Rent – How much rent is to be paid and the frequency of payment.

- Duration – An AST can be for any length of time. I would always suggest a tenancy of six months as the tenant has the right to run the duration of the tenancy unless there is a breach on either party. See below.

- Running expenses – It sets out who is liable for the running expenses of the property.

- Tenant obligations – It details the tenant's obligations to the property and the landlord, such as maintenance, not to sublet, informing the landlord of problems in good time, and reporting damage.

ENGLAND & WALES
ASSURED SHORTHOLD TENANCY AGREEMENT

Notes for Guidance		
Insert date of agreement.	Dated	_____
The address of the property to be let. For shared properties, be sure to identify clearly the tenant's room or part of the property, e.g. by giving it a number.	The Property (hereinafter called 'the Property')	_____ _____ _____ _____
The landlord should give here an address in England and Wales.	The Landlord (hereinafter called 'the Landlord')	_____ of _____ _____
		This is the Landlord's address for service of notices until the Tenant is notified of a different address in England and Wales.
Insert full name(s), and address(es) (if relevant) of every tenant.	The Tenant (hereinafter called 'the Tenant')	_____ of _____ _____
		Where the Tenant consists of more than one person, they will all have joint and several liability under this agreement (this means that they will each be liable for **all** sums due under this Agreement, not just liable for a proportionate part).
Insert name and address of guarantor. Delete if none.	The Guarantor (hereinafter called 'the Guarantor')	_____ of _____ _____
Insert period of term in weeks/months and date tenancy begins. * *Delete as applicable depending on whether rent is to be paid monthly or weekly.*	The Term	_____ beginning on _____('**the fixed period**') The tenancy will then continue, still subject to the terms and conditions set out in this Agreement, from **month to month/week to week** * from the end of this fixed period unless or until the Tenant gives notice that he wishes to end the Agreement as set out in clause 4 overleaf, or the Landlord serves on the Tenant a notice under Section 21 of the Housing Act 1988, or a new form of Agreement is entered into, or this Agreement is ended by consent or a court order.
* *Delete as applicable. NB If rent is paid weekly, a rent book must be provided to the tenant.*	The Rent	£_____ per calendar **month/week** * by way of standing order into the Landlord's bank, details of which have been provided to the Tenant*.
† *If paid weekly, give the day in the week, e.g. Monday.*	The Payment Date	The first payment to be made on the signing of this Agreement. All subsequent payments to be made **monthly/weekly** * in advance on the _____ **day of the month/** _____ **of each week** *†.
NB The deposit should not exceed two months' rent.	The Deposit	£ _____ The deposit to be held as security by the Landlord for any loss or damage caused by the breach of any of the Tenant's obligations under this Agreement, or any sum repayable by the Landlord to the Local Authority in respect of Housing Benefit paid direct to the Landlord. See also clause 5 overleaf.
Delete this section if there is no inventory.	The Inventory	Being the list of the Landlord's possessions at the Property and details of condition which has been signed by the Landlord and the Tenant, a copy of which is annexed hereto.

This Agreement is intended to create an assured shorthold tenancy as defined in the Housing Act 1988, as amended by the Housing Act 1996, and the provisions for the recovery of possession by the Landlord in that Act apply accordingly. The Tenant understands that the Landlord will be entitled to recover possession of the Property at the end of the Term.

Delete paragraph if whole property is being let.

[Under this Agreement, the Tenant will have exclusive occupation of his designated room and will share with other occupiers of the Property the use and facilities of the Property (including such bathroom, toilet, kitchen and sitting room facilities as may be at the Property).]

Delete sentence which does not apply.

1. The Tenant's obligations:

1.1 To pay the Rent at the times and in the manner aforesaid.

1.2 [To pay all charges in respect of any electric, gas, water, telephonic and televisual services used at or supplied to the Property and Council Tax or any similar property tax that might be charged in addition to or replacement of it during the Term.] [To make a proportionate contribution to the costs of all charges in respect of any electric, gas, water and telephone or televisual services used at or supplied to the Property and Council Tax or any similar property tax that might be charged in addition to or replacement of it during the Term.]

1.3 To keep the items on the Inventory and the interior of the Property in a good and clean state and condition and not damage or injure the Property or the items on the Inventory (fair wear and tear excepted).

1.4 To yield up the Property and the items on the Inventory (if any) at the end of the Term in the same clean state and condition it/they was/were in at the beginning of the Term (but the Tenant will not be responsible for fair wear and tear caused during normal use of the Property, and the items on the Inventory or for any damage covered by and recoverable under the insurance policy effected by the Landlord under clause 2.2).

1.5 Not make any alteration or addition to the Property nor without the Landlord's prior written consent (consent not to be withheld unreasonably) do any redecoration or painting of the Property.

1.6 Not do anything on or at the Property which:

1.6.1 may be or become a nuisance or annoyance to any other occupiers of the Property or owners or occupiers of adjoining or nearby premises

1.6.2 is illegal or immoral

1.6.3 may in any way affect the validity of the insurance of the Property and the items listed on the Inventory or cause an increase in the premium payable by the Landlord.

1.7 Not without the Landlord's prior consent (consent not to be withheld unreasonably) allow or keep any pet or any kind of animal at the Property.

1.8 Not use or occupy the Property in any way whatsoever other than as a private residence.

1.9 Not to assign, sublet, charge or part with or share possession or occupation of the Property (but see clause 4.1 below).

1.10 To allow the Landlord or anyone with the Landlord's written permission to enter the Property at reasonable times of the day to inspect its condition and state of repair, carry out any necessary repairs and gas inspections, or during the last month of the Term, show the Property to prospective new tenants, provided the Landlord has given 24 hours' prior written notice (except in emergency).

1.11 To pay the Landlord's reasonable costs reasonably incurred as a result of any breaches by the Tenant of his obligations under this Agreement.

1.12 To pay interest at the rate of 4% above the Bank of England base rate from time to time prevailing on any rent or other money due from the Tenant which remains unpaid for more that 14 days, interest to be paid from the date the payment fell due until payment.

1.13 To provide the Landlord with a forwarding address when the tenancy comes to an end and to remove all rubbish and all personal items (including the Tenant's own furniture and equipment) from the Property before leaving.

2 The Landlord's obligations:

2.1 The Landlord agrees that the Tenant may live in the Property without unreasonable interruption from the Landlord or any person rightfully claiming under or in trust for the Landlord.

2.2 To insure the Property and the items listed on the Inventory and use all reasonable efforts to arrange for any damage caused by an insured risk to be remedied as soon as possible and to provide a copy of the insurance policy to the Tenant.

2.3 To keep in repair

2.3.1 the structure and exterior of the Property (including drains, gutters and external pipes)

2.3.2 the installations at the Property for the supply of water, gas and electricity and for sanitation (including basins, sinks, baths and sanitary conveniences), and

2.3.3 the installations at the Property for space heating and heating water.

2.4 But the Landlord will not be required to:

2.4.1 carry out works for which the Tenant is responsible by virtue of his duty to use the Property in a tenant-like manner

2.4.2 reinstate the Property in the case of damage or destruction if the insurers refuse to pay out the insurance money due to anything the Tenant has done or failed to do

2.4.3 rebuild or reinstate the Property in the case of destruction or damage of the Property by a risk not covered by the policy of insurance effected by the Landlord.

3 Guarantor

If there is a Guarantor, he guarantees that the Tenant will keep to his obligations in this agreement. The Guarantor agrees to pay on demand to the Landlord any money lawfully due to the Landlord by the Tenant.

4 Ending this Agreement

4.1 The Tenant cannot normally end this Agreement before the end of the Term. However, after the first three months of the Term, if the Tenant can find a suitable alternative tenant, and provided this alternative tenant is acceptable to the Landlord (the Landlord's approval not to be unreasonably withheld) the Tenant may give notice to end the tenancy on a date at least one month from the date that such approval is given by the Landlord. On the expiry of such notice, provided that the Tenant pays to the Landlord the reasonable expenses reasonably incurred by the Landlord in granting the necessary approval and in granting any new tenancy to the alternative tenant, the tenancy shall end.

4.2 If the Tenant stays on after the end of the fixed Term, his tenancy will continue but will run from month to month (a 'periodic tenancy'). This periodic tenancy can be ended by the Tenant giving at least one month's written notice to the Landlord, the notice to expire at the end of a rental period.

4.3 If at any time

4.3.1 any part of the Rent is outstanding for 21 days after becoming due (whether formally demanded or not) and/or

4.3.2 there is any breach, non-observance or non-performance by the Tenant of any covenant or other term of this Agreement which has been notified in writing to the Tenant and the Tenant has failed within a reasonable period of time to remedy the breach and/or pay reasonable compensation to the Landlord for the breach and/or

4.3.3 any of the grounds set out as Grounds 2, 8 or Grounds 10-15 (inclusive) (which relate to breach of any obligation by a Tenant) contained in the Housing Act 1988 Schedule 2 apply

the Landlord may recover possession of the Property and this Agreement shall come to an end. The Landlord retains all his other rights in respect of the Tenant's obligations under this Agreement. Note that if anyone is living at the Property or if the tenancy is an assured or assured shorthold tenancy then the Landlord must obtain a court order for possession before re-entering the Property. This clause does not affect the Tenant's rights under the Protection from Eviction Act 1977.

5 The Deposit

5.1 The Deposit will be held by the Landlord and will be refunded to the Tenant at the end of the Term (however it ends) at the forwarding address provided to the Landlord but less any reasonable deductions properly made by the Landlord to cover any reasonable costs incurred or losses caused to him by any breaches of the obligations in this Agreement by the Tenant. No interest will be payable to the Tenant in respect of the deposit money.

5.2 The Deposit shall be repayable to the Tenant as soon as reasonably practicable, however the Landlord shall not be bound to return the deposit until he is satisfied that no money is repayable to the Local Authority if the Tenant has been in receipt of Housing Benefit, and until after he has had a reasonable opportunity to assess the reasonable cost of any repairs required as a result of any breaches of his obligations by the Tenant or other sums properly due to the Landlord under clause 5.1. However, the Landlord shall not, save in exceptional circumstances, retain the Deposit for more than one month after the end of the tenancy.

5.3 If at any time during the Term the Landlord is obliged to deduct from the Deposit to satisfy the reasonable costs occasioned by any breaches of the obligations of the Tenant, the Tenant shall make such additional payments as are necessary to restore the full amount of the Deposit.

6 Other provisions

6.1 The Landlord hereby notifies the Tenant under Section 48 of the Landlord & Tenant Act 1987 that any notices (including notices in proceedings) should be served upon the Landlord at the address stated with the name of the Landlord overleaf.

6.2 For stamp duty purposes, the Landlord and the Tenant confirm that there is no previous agreement to which this Agreement gives effect.

6.3 The Landlord shall be entitled to have and retain keys for all the doors to the Property but shall not be entitled to use these to enter the Property without the consent of the Tenant (save in an emergency).

6.4 Any notices or other documents shall be deemed served on the Tenant during the tenancy by either being left at the Property or by being sent to the Tenant at the Property by first-class post. If notices or other documents are served on the Tenant by post they shall be deemed served on the day after posting.

6.5 Any person other than the Tenant who pays all or part of the rent due under this Agreement to the Landlord shall be deemed to have made such payment as agent for and on behalf of the Tenant which the Landlord shall be entitled to assume without enquiry.

6.6 Any personal items left behind at the end of the tenancy after the Tenant has vacated (which the Tenant has not removed in accordance with clause 1.13 of this Agreement) shall be considered abandoned if they have not been removed within 14 days of written notice to the Tenant from the Landlord or if the Landlord has been unable to trace the Tenant by taking reasonable steps to do so. After this period the Landlord may remove or dispose of the items as he thinks fit. The Tenant shall be liable for the reasonable disposal costs which may be deducted from the proceeds of sale (if any), and the Tenant shall remain liable for any balance. Any net proceeds of sale will be dealt with in the same way as the Deposit as set out in clause 5.2 above.

6.7 In the event of damage to or destruction of the Property by any of the risks insured against by the Landlord the Tenant shall be relieved from payment of the Rent to the extent that the Tenant's use and enjoyment of the Property is thereby prevented and from performance of its obligations as to the state and condition of the Property to the extent of and so long as there prevails such damage or destruction (except to the extent that the insurance is prejudiced by any act or default of the Tenant).

6.8 Where the context so admits:

6.8.1 The 'Landlord' includes the persons from time to time entitled to receive the Rent.

6.8.2 The 'Tenant' includes any persons deriving title under the Tenant.

6.8.3 The 'Property' includes any part or parts of the Property and all of the Landlord's fixtures and fittings at or upon the Property.

6.8.4 All references to the singular shall include the plural and vice versa and any obligations or liabilities of more than one person shall be joint and several (this means that they will each be liable for *all* sums due under this Agreement, not just liable for a proportionate part) and an obligation on the part of a party shall include an obligation not to allow or permit the breach of that obligation.

6.8.5 All references to 'he', 'him' and 'his' shall be taken to include 'she', 'her' and 'hers'.

ENGLAND & WALES

Insert here any additional terms you would like incorporated into the Agreement.	Additional provisions (if any)	_____
		_____
		_____
		_____
		_____
		_____
		_____
		_____
		_____
		_____
		_____
		_____
		_____
		_____
		_____
		_____
		_____
		_____
		_____
		_____

Landlord signs here	Landlord's signature	_____
Witness (if any) signs here	Witness's signature	_____
All tenants sign here	Tenant's signature(s)	_____
		_____
		_____
		_____
Witness (if any) signs here	Witness's signature	_____
Guarantor signs here (if any)	Guarantor's signature	_____
Witness signs here	Witness's signature	_____

Fig 7.1. Example Assured Shorthold Tenancy Agreement

- Landlord obligations – It details the landlord's obligations to the property and the tenant, such as privacy and timeliness of repairs. Under sections 11 to 16 of the Landlord and Tenant Act 1985, a landlord is obliged to keep in repair the structure and exterior of the house; the water, electricity and gas supplies; and the heating. If the tenanted property forms part of a larger building (e.g. a block of flats) which the landlord owns or controls, the landlord will also be responsible for the repair of the common parts and installations.

Both the tenant and the landlord have to sign, with both signatures, witnessed by an independent third party.

An AST must be compliant with The Unfair Terms in Consumer Contracts Regulations 1999, otherwise it will be deemed invalid. The Office of Fair Trading has issued a document called *Guidance on Unfair Terms in Tenancy Agreements*. This can be bought from the OFT or downloaded for free from their website at www.oft.gov.uk. This directive protects tenants from any clauses which exclude or limit their rights. For example, the introduction of penalty clauses which do not reflect genuine cost to the landlord or general costs which are not specified.

Ready-drafted ASTs are available from Lawpack, and an example is provided on pages 53 to 56; visit www.lawpack.co.uk for details. Landlords can obtain further information about their legal rights and obligations at www.landlordlaw.co.uk, run by specialist solicitor and Lawpack author Tessa Shepperson.

3. An eviction order

To commence the legal process of evicting a tenant, the landlord must have a 'ground' for eviction and serve the proper notice on the tenant before any court action is started.

There are two categories for grounds of possession: mandatory and discretionary. It is advisable only to evict on mandatory grounds as the judge will have no option but to grant an order for possession. With regard to discretionary grounds, the tenant can defend the claim by possibly obtaining Legal Aid, which could end up being costly for you should you lose.

Here are the two most common mandatory grounds for possession. If the tenancy is an assured shorthold tenancy, the landlord can serve a Housing Act 1988 section 21 notice after the fixed term has expired. Alternatively, if the tenant is in rent arrears of 8 weeks/two months, both at the time of the service of the notice (a section 8 notice) and the court hearing, ground 8 in Schedule 2 of the Housing Act 1988 can be used.

It is recommended that you hand the notices to the tenant personally. Do make sure that your paperwork is completely accurate, as judges are wary of granting possession orders and will refuse to do so on the grounds of mistakes.

At no time can a landlord evict a tenant in any way other than through the courts. To manhandle him out of the property is a criminal offence.

To be honest, eviction is an extremely complicated process. As a result, we advise you always to consult a solicitor, but if you do want to find out more about the subject, then do read Lawpack's *Residential Lettings Guide* or speak to your Citizens Advice Bureau. If you do decide to act on your own behalf, the Court Service do publish a series of leaflets, which are available at County Courts or online at www.courtservice.gov.uk.

We have to face a reality, though. The procedure is stressful and will take a long time. It can potentially involve you losing six months' rent and will include court and solicitors' fees plus the threat of damage to your property.

To avoid such a battle, you could offer to pay your tenant to leave. This option could be cheaper. I would suggest one month's rent being fair. This will pay the deposit for their next property.

Try to initiate a friendly separation. Do not add fuel to an already fiery situation by losing your temper and threatening immediate court action. Statistically only three per cent of tenants tend to be bad tenants – bad tenants being tenants who have no intention of paying the rent, not tenants who lose their job and can't pay their rent. If a tenant loses his job it is more than likely that he is going to get another job. If he has been a relatively good payer of the rent, be patient with him.

In my experience, I would say that the three per cent statistic is right. The majority of people wish to settle in a home and feel secure. The best way for them to feel secure is to pay their rent on time.

Insurers

You will have to enter legal contracts with insurance companies to cover you against certain risks. Your insurance will only ever be valid if you have originally told the truth on your proposal form when obtaining the insurance. The main insurances you will take out when investing in property will be:

- **Buildings insurance:** The insurance you pay to cover the property against fire, vandalism, water damage or weather damage.

- **Contents insurance:** This is insurance for items such as carpets, furniture and other fittings that you have provided for the property.

- **Rental guarantee:** This is insurance against your tenant defaulting on the rental payments.

- **Emergency assistance:** This insurance will cover the costs of any emergency repairs that have to be carried out, including all call-out charges.

When filling out the form they will ask you about previous claims. If you have any previous claims, then reveal them. If you do have to make a claim and you have not told them about a previous claim, they do not have to pay out. It is very easy for them to find out if you have had a claim as they have a central register of all claims paid out.

If you do lie and they catch you out, you will find it difficult to get insurance in the future, as you may be put on a blacklist which is accessible to all insurers.

Do not rely on general household insurance for a residential property and do make sure that the insurance company knows your property is rented. There are certain policies which do exclude asylum seekers, Housing Benefit claimants or students as tenants so check each clause carefully.

Letting agents

If you do decide to use a letting agent, then you have to read their terms and conditions very carefully. Watch for:

- **Timeliness of payment:** Check to see how soon the letting agent has to hand over the money, once the tenant has received it. I would not accept any period longer than three days.

- **Get-out clauses:** If you decide to use the letting agent no longer, check to see how easy it is to get out. One agent tried to sue me for all the lost commission he would have earned, even though I was now collecting the rent! If you want to use a letting agent at first and then take over in six months, inform the letting agent of this intention. You may be able to strike a deal where you have a realistically priced option to get out of the contract.

Regulatory

There are there main regulations governing the renting of properties:

1. Gas safety
2. Electrical safety
3. Fire resistance

1. Gas safety

If there is gas at the property, then you have to get a landlord's safety record from a CORGI (Council for Registered Gas Installers)-registered engineer. They will inspect:

- The central heating boiler
- Oven and hob
- Gas fire
- Gas meters

The property needs to be inspected annually and a copy of the certificate needs to be presented to the tenant at the start of the tenancy and each year thereafter.

If you do not get one of these certificates and someone suffers or even dies from carbon monoxide poisoning, you could face a hefty fine and imprisonment. The guilt will be even worse.

For further advice, contact the Health and Safety Executive which produces the Health & Safety Executive Code of Practice and Guidance. The obligations of landlords are summarised in the leaflet *A Guide to Landlords' Duties* available free. Also, go online at www.hse.gov.uk.

2. Electrical safety

A yearly inspection is needed for all electrical appliances supplied with the property by an NICEIC (National Inspection Council for Electrical Installation) contractor. Basically anything electrical will need to be examined and passed by the NICEIC contractor.

So it's quite obvious – keep the number of electrical items to a minimum! The fewer electrical items you supply, the less there is likely to go wrong. You don't need your tenant ringing you up at 6am complaining about the kettle not working.

There is no NICEIC certificate issued, but an inspection will cover you from being sued if any electrical appliance were to harm your tenants or their guests.

Electrical items also must comply with the Plugs and Sockets Safety Regulations. This should not be an issue if the appliances were purchased recently.

3. Fire resistance

All upholstered furniture must comply with the Furniture and Furnishings (Fire Safety) Regulations 1988. You can tell if the furniture is compliant because there will be a label in the cushioning. Any furniture purchased after 1990 will automatically comply with all fire regulations.

Although not a legal requirement, I would recommend that smoke alarms be installed in rented properties to cover you against any negligence claim if you were to be sued.

All-encompassing

You will also be legally bound by the normal all-encompassing laws of the land which apply to us all. These include:

1. The law of tort – negligence and personal injury
2. Criminal law

1. The law of tort

Even though you may have all the safety records in place, you still owe a duty of care to your tenant and anyone that enters your property. If it can be shown that you were negligent in any way, you could be sued and ordered to pay damages.

As a landlord, you are liable for any damages if the following apply:

i)   your tenant or anyone entering your investment property suffers an injury; and

ii) you owed a duty of care to the person entering your investment property who suffered the personal injury; and

iii) you breached that duty of care.

So for example if Zak, the landlord, failed to fix the cooker socket in the kitchen and the tenant's guest, Liz, suffered an electric shock burn, then Zak would be liable to compensate Liz for her injury.

This is because:

i)   Liz suffered injury;

ii) Zak owed a duty of care, as it is realistically expected that a tenant would invite a guest into their property;

iii) Zak breached that duty of care, as he had not fixed the socket when asked to by the tenant.

2. Criminal law

Even if your tenant hasn't paid you any rent for two months, you cannot 'send the boys round'. Threatening your tenant or being violent to your tenant because he hasn't paid you any rent is no justification for your behaviour in the eyes of the law.

Harassment legislation entitles the tenant to bring civil proceedings himself against you for an injunction and/or damages. Alternatively, the tenant can complain to the local authorities, who may proceed with criminal prosecution, which may end up in a fine or two years' imprisonment if you are found guilty.

Examples of action which are seen as harassment are threats of/or actual violence, disconnection of gas and electricity and entering the property without the consent of the tenant.

Should you be accused of harassment, stop visiting or contacting the tenant by telephone. Consider approaching them through a solicitor and always contact them in writing. Signed and dated copies of correspondence should be kept at all times.

In the end, remember, it's only money! This is the phrase I say to myself when I get stressed when a tenant 'does a runner' and leaves me with £1,500 owing. As I said in the Introduction, you have to be a responsible person and realise that if you want to take investing in property seriously, you have to act lawfully in every way.

8 Reference chapter

In this chapter you will find all the addresses, phone numbers and websites you will need to get started in property investment. This chapter covers:

i) 100 per cent LTV mortgage providers

100 per cent mortgage providers can fund the whole purchase price of a property. Some providers below also refund the valuation and legal fees. Some offer in excess of 100 per cent. They also offer up to five times your salary plus your partner's salary as total borrowings. These lenders are giving it to you on a plate! Read the notes on each lender to find out how much they lend.

Lender: **Bank of Scotland Mortgage Direct**

Rate: 4.99% – 31 October 2005, then variable rate (5.55% currently)

Set up costs:

Mortgage Indemnity Premium: £3,000.00
Arrangement fee: £300.00
Less cashback: Nil
Net costs: £3,300.00
Other incentives: None

Conditions:

Early redemption penalty: 2% and 1% until 31 October 2005, £150 administration charge thereafter
Conditional Insurances: None
How much you can borrow:
Single income – 3.25 times
Joint incomes – 3.25 times main income

plus 1 times second income or 2.75 times joint income

Additional features:

Enhanced income multiples available for professionals: doctors, dentists, pharmacists, actuaries, solicitors/barristers, chartered surveyors, chartered accountants, architects and veterinary surgeons. No arrangement fee will be charged for cases direct with lender.

Lender: **Direct Line Mortgages**

Rate: 3.99% – 6 months, then 4.9% – 2.5 years, then variable rate (4.96% currently)

Monthly costs:

Initial monthly payment: £526.79
Monthly payment at lenders Standard
Variable Rate: £581.68

Set up costs:

Mortgage Indemnity Premium: £375.00
Arrangement fee: Nil
Less cashback: Nil
Net costs: £375.00
Other incentives: Valuation fees refunded

Conditions:

Early redemption penalty: 3 months within 3 years
Conditional Insurances: None
How much you can borrow:
Single income – 3 times
Joint incomes – 3 times main income plus 1 times second income or 2.5 times joint income

Additional features:

Scheme is a 0.97% discount for the first 6 months then 0.06% discount for the remainder of the discount period. Ability to overpay, underpay and take payment holidays. Lender charges interest on a daily basis. Lender's acceptance is based upon affordability. The income multiples shown above are for guidance only.

Lender: **Nat West**

Rate: 4.49% – 31 August 2005, then variable rate (5.59% currently)

Monthly costs:

Initial monthly payment: £554.72
Monthly payment at lenders Standard
Variable Rate: £618.83

Set up costs:

Mortgage Indemnity Premium: £1,030.00
Arrangement fee: Nil
Less cashback: Nil
Net costs: £1,030.00
Other incentives: None

Conditions:

Early redemption penalty: None
Conditional Insurances: None
How much you can borrow:
Single income – 3.25 times
Joint incomes – 3.25 times main income plus 1 times second income or 2.75 times joint income

Additional features:

Will not lend in Northern Ireland. 1.1% discount. No valuation fee. Interest calculated daily. Increased income multiples for professionals of up to 5 times professional salary plus 1 times second salary, or up to 2.75 times joint salary for joint applications. Applicants must be a fully qualified member of one of the following professions: medical doctors, pharmacists, opticians, dentists, vets, solicitors and accountants (minimum salary £20,000, minimum age 23 and must meet all standard affordability guidelines).

Lender: **Northern Rock**

Rate: 3.89% – 1 October 2004, then 5.35% – 1 October 2006, then variable rate (5.49% currently)

Set up costs:

Mortgage Indemnity Premium: N/A
Arrangement fee: £495.00
Less cashback: Nil
Net costs: £495.00
Other incentives: None

Conditions:

Early redemption penalty: 2% of original loan on full redemption within 3 years
Conditional Insurances: None
How much you can borrow:
Single income – 3.5 times
Joint incomes – 3.5 times main income plus 1 times second income or 2.75 times joint income

Additional features:

Will not lend in Northern Ireland. Free accident, sickness and unemployment cover for 3 months. Up to 85% loan secured and 30% as an unsecured loan. Scheme is fixed until 1 October 2004, then Bank of England base rate (currently 3.5%) plus 1.85% until 1 October 2006. Lender charges interest on a daily basis. Ability to overpay, underpay and take payment holidays.

Lender: **Royal Bank of Scotland**

Rate: 4.46% – 1 August 2005, then variable rate (5.59% currently)

Monthly costs:

Initial monthly payment: £553.02
Monthly payment at lenders Standard Variable Rate: £618.83

Set up costs:

Mortgage Indemnity Premium: £1,200.00
Arrangement fee: Nil
Less cashback: Nil
Net costs: £1,200.00
Other incentives: None

Conditions:

Early redemption penalty: None
Conditional Insurances: None
How much you can borrow:
Single income – 3.25 times
Joint incomes – 3.25 times main income plus 1 times second income or 2.75 times joint income

Additional features:

1.63% discount off bank's 100% variable rate (currently 6.09%), then after 1 August 2005 reverts to Standard Variable Rate. Lender charges interest on a daily basis. Free accident, sickness and unemployment cover for 3 months. Higher income multiples for professionals.

Lender: **Sainsbury's Bank**

Rate: 4.7%

Monthly costs:

Initial monthly payment: £566.68
Monthly payment at lenders Standard Variable Rate: £566.68

Set up costs:

Mortgage Indemnity Premium: £3,000.00
Arrangement fee: Nil
Less cashback: Nil
Net costs: £3,000.00
Other incentives: None

Conditions:

Early redemption penalty: None
Conditional Insurances: None
How much you can borrow:
Single income – 3 times
Joint incomes – 3 times main income plus 1
times second income or 2.5 times joint
income

Additional features:

Ability to overpay, underpay and take
payment holidays. Lender charges interest
on a daily basis. The flexible options are
exercised by calling Sainsbury's Bank
Customer Services. A preset limit is placed
on each mortgage account at the outset,
equivalent to the original loan plus 5% of
the valuation of the property. The
'overpayments' and '10 repayments a year'
flexible options may be exercised
immediately, the other flexible options may
be exercised after 3 or 24 monthly
repayments depending on the original loan
to value and provided there has been no
breach of the mortgage terms and
conditions. Underpayment can be made or
further advances taken up to the preset
limit. Payments can be stopped for a
maximum of 6 monthly instalments or up
to the preset limit, whichever is less. Any
previous overpayments or lump sum
payments into the account can also be
withdrawn. New customers receive 30,000

free Sainsbury's Nectar points every year
(in December).

Lender: **Scottish Widows Bank**

Rate: 3.89% – 30 September 2004, then
4.1% – 30 September 2005, then 4.8% – 30
September 2008, then variable rate (4.9%
currently)

Monthly costs:

Initial monthly payment: £521.30
Monthly payment at lenders Standard
Variable Rate: £578.20

Set up costs:

Mortgage Indemnity Premium: N/A
Arrangement fee: £295.00
Less cashback: Nil
Net costs: £295.00
Other incentives: Valuation fees refunded –
maximum £250. Legal fees refunded –
maximum £150

Conditions:

Early redemption penalty: 3% of amount
until 30 September 2008 plus legal and
valuation fees reclaimed within 3 years
Conditional Insurances: None
How much you can borrow:
Single income – 3.5 times
Joint incomes – 3.5 times main income plus
1 times second income or 3.5 times joint
income

Additional features:

Will not lend in Northern Ireland. Graduate
Mortgage – must be over 21 years old and
educated to at least degree standard from a
recognised UK university within last 7
years. Must have been in permanent

employment in the UK in the preceding 12 months prior to application, (not currently serving a probationary period). Minimum term 5 years, maximum 40 years or expected retirement age. Cheque book facility available. Valuation fee refunded on completion. Lender charges interest on a daily basis. Arrangement fee shown is a non-refundable booking fee. Graduate Mortgage – lending available up to 102% LTV, additional 2% is on secured basis over a maximum 10-year period. Capital repayments up to 10% allowed each year without penalty (minimum £1,000).

Lender: **Yorkshire Building Society**

Rate: 3.5% – 1 year, then 4.25% – 1 year, then variable rate (5.25% currently)

Set up costs:

Mortgage Indemnity Premium: £3,000.00
Arrangement fee: Nil
Less cashback: Nil
Net costs: £3,000.00
Other incentives: Valuation fees and legal fees refunded

Conditions:

Early Redemption Penalty: 3% within 2 years
Conditional Insurances: None
How much you can borrow:
Single Income – 3.5 times
Joint Incomes – 3.5 times main income plus 2.2 times second income

Additional features:

Ability to overpay, underpay and take payment holidays. Lender charges interest on a daily basis. Free mortgage payment protection insurance for first 6 months. Lender will use affordability calculation to calculate potential loan size – refer to lender for details. Lender's acceptance is based upon affordability – the income multiples shown above are for guidance only. Minimum age 25. Minimum loan for loans above 95% is £50,000. Scheme is Bank of England base rate (currently 3.5%) for 1 year then plus 0.75% for year 2. £350 contribution towards legal fees on completion.

ii) Buy-to-let mortgage providers

If you wish to approach a lender direct then you can refer to this list. The mortgage companies listed below will fund anywhere between 50-85% of the purchase price of an investment residential property. Some of these lenders require that you are employed or earning in excess of a certain limit. I have listed them in descending LTVs. Thus the higher up the list your choice of lender is, the greater the buying power you have.

85 per cent LTV

Lender: **Birmingham Midshires**

Tel: (01902) 302 591
Website: www.bm-solutions.co.uk
Email: lending@birminghammidshires.co.uk

Arrangement fee: £299.00
Repayment options: Any
Life insurance required: No
Acceptable areas: UK

Notes:

1. Minimum valuation – £40,000 (£75,000 in London).
2. Limit of 10 buy-to-let properties per borrower up to a limit of £100,000.
3. Rental income can be used if 125% of monthly mortgage payments.
4. Holiday lets acceptable.
5. Multiple lets including student lets are not acceptable.
6. Refer to lender for terms for expatriates.
7. Intermediary only.
8. Lender will allow 1satisfied CCJ and arrears of £250 registered within the last 2 years.
9. 0.76% discount.
10. Minimum declared income – £10,000 per annum.

Lender: **Bristol & West**

Tel: (0845) 300 8000
Website: www.bristol-west.co.uk

Arrangement fee: Nil
Repayment options: Any
Life insurance required: No
Acceptable areas: England & Wales

Notes:

1. Minimum valuation of any property – £30,000.
2. DSS tenants are allowed.
3. No first time buyers.
4. Anticipated rent must be greater, or equal to, 125% of interest payment based on 9% charge rate.
5. Minimum income of £15,000 required.

6. Maximum of 5 properties per applicant allowed – total borrowing of £500,000.
7. Borrowers must be over 25.
8. Ability to overpay, underpay and take payment holidays.
9. Scheme is Bank of England base rate (currently 4%) plus 0.25%.
10. Booking fee of £399 is payable.
11. Employed applicants must produce their last month's payslip and an employer's reference.
12. Self-employed applicants must produce the agreed tax assessments from the latest year; the latest year's audited accounts prepared by a chartered, certified or authorised public accountant; and a letter from a chartered, certified or authorised public accountant confirming the applicant's salary or share of profit.

Lender: **Freedom Finance Mortgages & Loans Ltd**

Tel: (01625) 416 000
Website: www.freedomfinance.co.uk

Arrangement fee: £500.00
Repayment options: Any
Life insurance required: No
Acceptable areas: England, Scotland, Wales & Northern Ireland

Notes:

1. Rental income must exceed 130% of mortgage repayments.
2. Up to 10 properties allowed (£250,000 per property).
3. Bank of England base rate (currently 4%) plus 2%.

4. Arrangement fee is 1% of loan.

Lender: **Future Mortgages Ltd**

Tel: (0800) 389 1221
Website: www.future-mortgages.co.uk
Email: sales@future-mortgages.co.uk

Arrangement fee: £149.00
Repayment options: Any
Life insurance required: No
Acceptable areas: England, Wales &
Scotland

Notes:

1. Minimum valuation of any property –
    £50,000 for London postcodes and
    £20,000 for other areas.

2. Minimum lease allowed – 25 years on
    maturity of mortgage.

3. Lending will be based on rental income
    being 1.25 times the gross monthly
    payment.

4. Loans above £200,001 charged an
    additional 0.5% on the interest rate and
    1% for loans below £25,001.

5. Lender charges an additional fee of
    £295 which is added to the loan on
    completion.

6. Lender requires a specialist letting
    report to be undertaken with cost of
    £50 being met by applicant.

7. Rate is LIBOR (currently 4%) plus a
    minimum of a 3% loading.

8. Lender will allow adverse credit – CCJs:
    any number to £3,000 and arrears of 3
    months in last 12 months (none in last
    3 months).

9. Maximum of 5 loans (4 rental and
    primary residence) – total £500,000.

10. Discharged bankrupts allowed within
    last 6 months but must provide last 3
    months' bank statements.

Lender: **Paragon Mortgages Ltd**

Tel: (0800) 375 777
Website: www.paragon-mortgages.co.uk
Email: mortgages@paragon-group.co.uk

Arrangement fee: £500.00
Repayment options: Any
Life insurance required: Yes
Acceptable areas: England, Wales &
Scotland

Notes:

1. Minimum valuation of any property –
    £33,333.

2. Minimum lease allowed – 40 years on
    maturity of mortgage.

3. Up to 50% of the rental income may be
    added to applicant's income, provided
    this does not exceed 20% of the
    individual's total income, although for
    more than one property, different
    lending rules apply.

4. DSS, council or student tenants
    allowed.

5. No ex-local authority, studio or shared
    ownership properties allowed.

6. Will lend to limited companies.

7. Arrangement fee of between £200-
    £1,000 charged depending on
    circumstances.

8. Lender allows non-status lending,
    usually to 65%, at a higher rate.

9. Scheme is LIBOR linked, plus 0.75% in the first year, and 1.75% thereafter.

10. Lender offers a free switch at any time to one of its new fixed or capped rates for applicants who have taken either the variable or LIBOR linked fares.

11. No upfront valuation fees.

12. Will consider single property divided into maximum of 20 units – minimum valuation £100,000.

13. Will consider single property divided into maximum of 10 units – minimum valuation £50,000.

14. Minimum age of applicants is 21.

80 per cent LTV

Lender: **Britannic Money plc**

Tel: (01372) 737 737
Website: www.britannicmoney.com
Email: info@britannicmoney.com

Arrangement fee: £500.00
Repayment options: Any
Life insurance required: Yes
Acceptable areas: National coverage

Notes:

1. Minimum valuation of any property – £40,000.

2. Minimum lease allowed – 30 years on maturity of mortgage.

3. Minimum fee charged £500.

4. Applicants must be residential homeowners (minimum 1 year).

5. The rental income must be at least equal to 130% of the monthly payment as calculated at the charging rate.

6. DSS, council or student tenants not allowed.

7. Curriculum Vitae required on all applicants.

8. Lender may advance more than the normal maximum if a suitable investment policy with a surrender value can be assigned.

9. Rate charged is LIBOR plus 1.4% loading.

10. Now available to UK expatriates at 70%.

11. Lender also offers self-certification of income facility to 80% LTV.

12. 0.75% discount for 2 years.

13. Refer to lender to consider multiple properties, portfolio cases only, up to £1 million at 80% loan to value and above £1 million by negotiation.

Lender: **Capital Home Loans Ltd**

Tel: (020) 7624 5118
Website: www.chlmortgages.co.uk

Arrangement fee: £500.00
Repayment options: Any
Life insurance required: No
Acceptable areas: Mainland England, Wales & Northern Ireland

Notes:

1. Minimum valuation of any property – £40,000 (minimum of £50,000 for 1 bedroom flats/maisonettes).

2. Minimum lease allowed – 35 years on maturity of mortgage.

3. Minimum arrangement fee – £300.

4. Applicants must be resident and paying UK tax for a minimum of 3 years.

5. Applicants must be existing homeowners with an outstanding

mortgage or be a limited company/property developer/ commercial landlord.

6. Rental income must be at least 150% of the mortgage interest.

7. DSS, council or student tenants not allowed.

8. Loans over £637,500 by negotiation.

9. Scheme is Bank of England base rate (currently 4%) plus 1.24%.

Lender: **Chelsea**

Tel: (0800) 291 291
Website: www.thechelsea.co.uk

Arrangement fee: £440.00
Repayment options: Any
Life insurance required: No
Acceptable areas: UK

Notes:

1. Scheme is standard variable rate (currently 5.69%) plus 0.25% with 2% discount for 6 months.

2. Anticipated rent must be greater, or equal to, 125% of interest payment based on standard variable rate.

3. Maximum of 5 properties per applicant allowed – total borrowing of £500,000.

4. Property must be self-contained and have no more than 5 bedrooms and no more than 1 kitchen.

5. The letting must be on the basis of a single letting on the entire property and be on an Assured Shorthold Tenancy. The term of the letting must be for no longer than 6 months. The property must be either vacant or have a pre-existing Assured Shorthold Tenancy

subject to a maximum tenancy of 6 months.

Lender: **Cheshire Building Society**

Tel: (0345) 550 555
Website: www.cheshirebs.co.uk

Arrangement fee: £295.00
Repayment options: Any
Life insurance required: No
Acceptable areas: England (including Isle of Wight) & Wales

Notes:

1. DSS, students and multiple tenants are not allowed.

2. Maximum of 3 properties.

3. The gross assured monthly rental income is to be at least 125% of the monthly mortgage payments based on Capital and Interest Standard Variable Rates.

4. Applicants must already own and occupy their own property.

5. Applicant's minimum income must be at least £20,000 (joint £30,000).

6. Applicant's minimum age is 25.

7. Loans over £250,000 by negotiation with lender.

8. Arrangement fee on loans above £100,000 up to £250,000 is £350, over £250,000 by negotiation.

9. Compulsory buildings insurance will be arranged for 3 years.

10. If property has been converted into individual flats, then maximum number of flats is 3. Minimum loan – £30,000 per flat.

11. Free valuation.

Lender: **Clydesdale Bank**

Tel: (0800) 419 000
Website: www.cbonline.co.uk

Arrangement fee: £500.00
Repayment options: Interest only
Life insurance required: No
Acceptable areas: England, Scotland & Wales

Notes:

1. Minimum valuation of any property – £12,500.
2. Minimum lease allowed – 6 months.
3. The lender will use an affordability calculation based on the anticipated rental income.
4. Minimum arrangement fee of £100.
5. Maximum of 3 properties per applicant allowed.
6. Booking fee – £200.

Lender: **Coventry Building Society**

Tel: (0845) 766 5522
Website: www.coventrybuildingsociety.co.uk
Email: csa@coventrybuildingsociety.co.uk

Arrangement fee: £400.00
Repayment options: Any
Life insurance required: No
Acceptable areas: England, Wales & mainland Scotland

Notes:

1. Property must be let on an Assured Shorthold Tenancy.
2. Not available to companies or partnerships.
3. Minimum annual income for main earner is £25,000.

4. Employed applicants must be in permanent employment and have been so continuously for 12 months.
5. Self-employed verified via last 2 years' accounts.
6. Flats in blocks of no more then 5 storeys allowed; maximum loan 75%.
7. Applicants must be aged 25 years or above.
8. Monthly rental must be at least 130% of monthly mortgage interest.
9. No studio flats or converted for multi-occupancy properties or student lets.
10. Maximum of 4 properties allowed; maximum loan of £500,000.
11. Discounted legal fees for remortgages – the £285 fee will be added on completion.
12. 1.5% discount.

Lender: **First Trust Bank**

Tel: (01232) 325 599
Website: www.firsttrustbank.co.uk

Arrangement fee: £295.00
Repayment options: Any
Life insurance required: No
Acceptable areas: Northern Ireland

Notes:

1. Scheme is Bank of England base rate (currently 4%) plus 1.75%.
2. Maximum term – 20 years.
3. Maximum 3 properties per customer.
4. Income based on 3 times single income plus 1 times or 2.5 times joint income plus 50% of rental income.
5. Lender charges interest on a daily basis.

Lender: **Ipswich Building Society**

Tel: (01473) 213 110
Website: www.ipswich-bs.co.uk
Email: enquiries@ipswichbuildingsociety.
co.uk

Arrangement fee: £195.00
Repayment options: Any
Life insurance required: No
Acceptable areas: England & Wales only

Notes:

1. Minimum lease allowed – 30 years on maturity of the mortgage.
2. DSS, council or student tenants not allowed.
3. Monthly rental income must be at least 130% of the monthly interest repayments.
4. Free valuation for existing members.
5. Up to 4 properties considered.
6. Properties must not be in multiple occupancy.
7. Letting must be on an unfurnished basis.
8. Lettings must not be to a company or business.
9. Assignment of the rental income is required.

Lender: **Kensington Mortgage Co.**

Tel: (020) 7376 0110
Website: www.kmc.co.uk

Arrangement fee: £395.00
Repayment options: Any
Life insurance required: No
Acceptable areas: Scotland, England & Wales only

Notes:

1. Minimum valuation of any property – £33,000.
2. Minimum lease allowed – 25 years on maturity of mortgage.
3. CCJs maximum – £5,000 (cleared or not).
4. Rate is lenders Standard Variable plus 2.5% or (remortgage at plus 3%).
5. DSS, council or student tenants not allowed.
6. Maximum of 6 loans allowed, to a total borrowing of £750,000.
7. Gross rental income must be 130% of the mortgage payment.
8. Higher rate for remortgage applicants.
9. Secured loan/rent arrears, 1 payment last 0-6 months, 3 payments last 7-12 months.
10. Involuntary arrangements satisfied at completion.
11. Bankruptcy, discharged 1 year before application.

Lender: **Leeds & Holbeck**

Tel: (0113) 225 7777
Website: www.leeds-holbeck.co.uk
Email: info@leeds-holbeck.co.uk

Arrangement fee: £399.00
Repayment options: Any
Life insurance required: No
Acceptable areas: Fully national

Notes:

1. Minimum valuation of any property – £50,000 (£85,000 for London postcodes and £70,000 for South East postcodes).

2. Rental income to be 130% of monthly mortgage payment calculated on an interest only basis.

3. Portfolio of 3 properties allowed.

4. Capital repayments up to 10% allowed each year without penalty.

Lender: **Legal & General Bank Ltd**

Tel: (0500) 666 555
Website: www.landg.com

Arrangement fee: £150.00
Repayment options: Interest only
Life insurance required: Yes
Acceptable areas: Fully national

Notes:

1. Minimum valuation of any property – £35,000.

2. Minimum lease allowed – 50 years on maturity of mortgage.

3. DSS and council not considered.

4. Scheme is 1%, 0.75%, then 0.5% discount in year 3.

5. Minimum annual gross income – £15,000.

6. Rental income to be a minimum of 130% of mortgage repayments.

7. Minimum age of applicants is 25.

8. No first time buyers, i.e. must have main residential mortgage.

9. Overpayments and drawdown facility.

10. £400 cashback.

11. Free valuation.

12. Lettings to student tenants allowed, providing there are no more then 5 bedrooms and no more then 7 tenants.

Lender: **Manchester Building Society**

Tel: (0161) 833 8885
Website: www.themanchester.co.uk
Email: info@themanchester.co.uk

Arrangement fee: £150.00
Repayment options: Any
Life insurance required: Yes
Acceptable areas: England & Wales

Notes:

1. Minimum valuation of any property – £50,000.

2. Minimum lease allowed – 50 years on maturity of mortgage.

3. DSS, council or student tenants are not allowed.

4. Arrangement fee waived if building insurance taken from lender.

5. Building insurance is compulsory in the first 3 years. If taken from society, then arrangement fee is not charged.

6. The mortgage size will be limited to a maximum of 6 times the annual rental income.

7. Mortgage indemnity is charged on loans above 75%. Call lender for details.

Lender: **Mortgage Express**

Tel: (0500) 111 130
Website: www.mortgage-express.co.uk
Email: arla@mortgage-express.co.uk

Arrangement fee: £325.00
Repayment options: Any
Life insurance required: No
Acceptable areas: National coverage

Notes:

1. Minimum valuation allowed – £33,333.

2. Minimum lease allowed – 25 years on maturity of the mortgage.

3. DSS, council or student tenants not allowed.

4. Applicants must have income, outside of rental income, of at least £20,000. However, the ability to repay the mortgage is based on the fact that the rental income must be at least 130% of the mortgage payment.

5. Lender offers facility to overpay and then drawdown funds as required.

6. Rate charged is linked to the Bank of England base rate (currently 4%) plus a loading of 1.5% .

7. Lender offers a non-status facility to all applicants at either 50%, 60% or 70% of the property value/price with a loading to the above rate.

8. Letting assessment fee of £60 will be made.

Lender: **National Counties**

Tel: (01372) 742 211
Website: www.ncbs.co.uk

Arrangement fee: £495.00
Repayment options: Any
Life insurance required: No
Acceptable areas: England & Wales and within predominantly residential areas

Notes:

1. Minimum valuation of any property – £55,000 for flats/maisonettes and £80,000 for houses/bungalows.

2. Minimum lease allowed – 40 years on maturity of mortgage.

3. DSS, council or student tenants not allowed.

4. The annual rental income must be at least 140% of the gross interest payable at completion.

5. Lender requires the applicant to be conversant with the letting market, having appointed a professional letting agent to manage the property.

6. Lender has general flexible attitude and may amend criteria slightly.

Lender: **NewWorld**

Tel: (0845) 845 4455
Website: www.mynewworld.com

Arrangement fee: £500.00
Repayment options: Interest only
Life insurance required: No
Acceptable areas: England & Wales

Notes:

1. Maximum loan (over £500,000) will be based on affordability.

2. Up to 75% of gross rental income allowed.

3. Property exclusions, flying freehold, freehold flats, vacant land and shared ownership schemes.

4. UK residents over 18 years old.

5. Self-employed will need 3 years' worth of statements of trading profits certified by an accountant.

6. Single or multiple borrowers (maximum of 4).

7. The capped rate detailed is the maximum amount you will pay under this scheme. Payments are calculated on the introductory rate or the Standard Variable Rate whichever is the lower.

8. Scheme is capped at 6.99%.

9. Booking fee of £295 applies.

Lender: **Royal Bank of Scotland**

Tel: (0800) 121 121
Website: www.royalbankscot.co.uk

Arrangement fee: £250.00
Repayment options: Any
Life insurance required: Yes
Acceptable areas: Nationwide

Notes:

1. Maximum of 2 properties per applicant allowed.
2. Maximum total value – £1 million.
3. Minimum fee is 0.5% plus £295.
4. Rental income must exceed 130% of mortgage repayments.
5. Lender will use affordability calculation to calculate potential loan size – refer to lender for details.
6. Ability to overpay and take payment holidays.
7. DSS or council tenants not allowed.
8. Maximum term of 25 years.

Lender: **Sainsbury's Bank**

Tel: (0500) 700 600
Website: www.sainsburysbank.co.uk

Arrangement fee: £250.00
Repayment options: Any
Life insurance required: Yes
Acceptable areas: Fully national

Notes:

1. Minimum valuation of any property – £60,000
2. Minimum lease allowed – 50 years on maturity of mortgage.

3. DSS, council, company or student tenants not considered.
4. Rate is Bank of England base rate (currently 4%) plus 1.5%.
5. The lender will use an affordability calculation based on the anticipated rental income.
6. Gross annual rental income must equate to at least 10% of the loan amount.
7. Maximum of 65% for non-UK residents.
8. Maximum of 5 properties allowed – 30% required for each property purchased.
9. Applicants must own and reside in own property (i.e. no first time buyers).
10. Maximum amount – £350,000 per customer.

Lender: **Scarborough Building Society**

Tel: (0870) 513 3149
Website: www.scarboroughbs.co.uk
Email: dmc@scarboroughbs.co.uk

Arrangement fee: £325.00
Repayment options: Any
Life insurance required: No
Acceptable areas: England & Wales

Notes:

1. Will not lend in Scotland or Northern Ireland.
2. 1.04% discount.
3. Income multiples 3 times main, plus 1 times second or 2.5 times joint income, also up to 50% of rental income on a standalone basis.
4. 1 property maximum.

5. Minimum age of applicant is 18.
6. Minimum valuation – £50,000.
7. Capital raising criteria for those applicants between 55 and 80, maximum 60% loan to value, minimum valuation £50,000, maximum term 25 years and maximum age at maturity – 80.

Lender: **Scottish Building Society**

Tel: (0131) 220 1111
Website: www.scottishbs.co.uk
Email: mailbox@scottishbldgsoc.co.uk

Arrangement fee: Nil
Repayment options: Any
Life insurance required: No
Acceptable areas: Scotland

Notes:

1. 1% discount.
2. Maximum of 3 properties per applicant allowed.
3. Maximum total borrowing must not exceed £250,000.
4. Total borrowing should not be more than 3 times prime income plus 50% of rental income plus second income or 2.5 times joint income plus 50% of rental income.
5. Maximum term – 40 years.
6. Flexible options; ability to make over and under payments and payment holidays.

Lender: **Scottish Widows**

Tel: (0845) 845 0829
Website: www.scottishwidows.co.uk

Arrangement fee: £250.00
Repayment options: Any
Life insurance required: Yes
Acceptable areas: Fully national

Notes:

1. Minimum valuation of any property – £37,500.
2. Minimum lease allowed – 30 years on maturity of mortgage.
3. DSS tenants not allowed.
4. Interest is charged on a daily basis, so the scheme is flexible and allows overpayments and drawdown of funds.
5. Confirmation to be received that applicant is not solely reliant on rental income. Non-property-related income must be £15,000 per annum or more.
6. Monthly rental income should be at least 130% of monthly payments.
7. Minimum age of applicants is 21.
8. Maximum of 3 properties.
9. Interest only loans up to 70% allowed where residential mortgage is already held or is being transferred to the Scottish Widows Bank.
10. Bank of England base rate (currently 4%) plus 1.5%.

Lender: **Shepshed Building Society**

Tel: (01509) 822 000
Website: www.theshepshed.co.uk

Arrangement fee: £150.00
Repayment options: Any
Life insurance required: No
Acceptable areas: Will only lend in Leicestershire and East Midlands area

Notes:

1. Minimum valuation of any property – please contact lender to discuss.

2. No leasehold properties allowed.

3. DSS, council or student tenants allowed.

4. Lender has no specific rules regarding rental income and mortgage repayment ratio.

5. Remortgage allowed; minimum loan allowed – £25,001.

6. Rate is standard variable plus 0.5%.

Lender: **Skipton Building Society**

Tel: (01756) 705 000
Website: www.skipton.co.uk

Arrangement fee: £125.00
Repayment options: Any
Life insurance required: No
Acceptable areas: England, Wales & Scotland

Notes:

1. Minimum valuation of any property – £40,000.

2. Minimum lease allowed – 50 years on maturity of the mortgage.

3. Minimum income or profit (before tax) must be £20,000 for main applicant, and the expected rental income must cover the mortgage interest by 1.5 times.

4. DSS or council tenants not allowed.

5. 0.3% discount.

6. Lender charges interest on a daily basis.

7. Applicant must be a current homeowner.

8. Interest calculated daily.

9. Maximum of 3 properties.

10. Capital raising allowed to fund other buy-to-let purchases.

11. Guarantors allowed with prior approval.

Lender: **Southern Pacific Mortgages Ltd**

Tel: (020) 7590 1500
Website: www.spml.co.uk

Arrangement fee: £395.00
Repayment options: Any
Life insurance required: No
Acceptable areas: Fully national

Notes:

1. Minimum valuation of any property – £30,000.

2. Minimum lease allowed – 25 years plus mortgage term.

3. DSS, council or student tenants not allowed.

4. Only available via brokers – call above number for broker in your area.

5. Up to 6 properties per person (maximum total borrowing – £1 million).

6. Lender uses standard income multiples. In addition, lender requires rental income to be 130% of the mortgage repayment.

7. Lender can allow loans of £10,000-£25,000 with loading to rate of 0.7%.

8. Will allow applicants to have had adverse credit history – loan to value and interest rate will be determined by applicant situation.

9. Scheme is LIBOR (currently 4%) plus 3.45% for purchase applications, and 3.95% for remortgage applications.

10. Mortgage indemnity charged on advances above 70% (at 5%).

Lender: **UCB Home Loans**

Tel: (0645) 401 400
Website: www.ucbhomeloans.co.uk
Email: direct@ucbhomeloans.co.uk

Arrangement fee: £495.00
Repayment options: Any
Life insurance required: No
Acceptable areas: UK

Notes:

1. Scheme is Bank of England base rate (currently 4%) plus 1.99% with a 1% discount for 3 years.

2. DSS, council or student tenants not allowed.

3. Income can be based on both personal and rental income.

4. Self-certification applicants welcome.

5. Applicants can borrow up to 3.25 plus 1 times income or 2.75 joint income plus up to 6.5 times annual rental income if intending to let.

6. Can purchase 2 properties in addition to main residence.

7. Main residence can be remortgaged to raise capital.

Lender: **UKCFG**

Tel: (01732) 763 660
Email: sevenoaks@mortgagesforbusiness. co.uk

Arrangement fee: £500.00
Repayment options: Any
Life insurance required: No
Acceptable areas: England, Wales & Scotland

Notes:

1. Minimum valuation of any property – £62,500.

2. Minimum lease allowed – 25 years on maturity of mortgage.

3. Gross rental income to exceed mortgage payment by 30%.

4. DSS, council or student tenants not allowed.

5. No ex-local authority, studio or bedsit property allowed.

6. Product only available via UK Commercial Funding Group members who are accredited to the NACFB and who may charge additional fees.

7. Rate reverts to Bank of England base rate (currently 4%) plus 1.5% for loans up to 75% and plus 1.75% for loans up to 80%.

8. Unlimited number of properties to maximum £1 million total loans.

Lender: **Verso**

Tel: (0845) 840 3020

Arrangement fee: £500.00
Repayment options: Any
Life insurance required: No
Acceptable areas: England, Wales & Scotland

Notes:

1. Minimum valuation of any property – £30,000.

2. Multiple properties allowed – maximum loan based on each property, not on total of portfolio.

3. Minimum age is 21.

4. Rental income to equal 125% of amount of mortgage calculated at 7%.

5. DSS, council, company lets, tenants with diplomatic immunity and multi-let properties are not allowed.

6. Only available through brokers.

7. Arrangement fee – 1% of advance (minimum £500).

8. An Assured Shorthold Tenancy for a maximum of 12 months.

9. Only 1 tenancy per property.

10. Applicants must be UK or EU nationals, resident and employed in the UK.

11. Verso may insist on the appointment of a suitably qualified letting agent.

12. Bank of England base rate (currently 4%) plus 0.98%.

Lender: **West Bromwich**

Tel: (0121) 580 6404
Website: www.westbrom.co.uk

Arrangement fee: £295.00
Repayment options: Any
Life insurance required: Yes
Acceptable areas: National coverage

Notes:

1. Minimum valuation of any property – £35,000.

2. Minimum lease allowed – 40 years on maturity of mortgage.

3. No ex-local authority or pre-1920 terraced property allowed.

4. DSS or council tenants not allowed.

5. Rent guarantee policy may be required.

6. Maximum of 3 properties allowed.

7. Rental income to be 150% of mortgage repayment.

8. 0.75% discount.

9. Capital repayments up to 10% allowed each year without penalty.

Lender: **Yorkshire Bank**

Tel: (0800) 202 122
Website: www.ybonline.co.uk

Arrangement fee: £500.00
Repayment options: Capital and Interest
Life insurance required: No
Acceptable areas: England & Wales

Notes:

1. Minimum valuation of any property – £12,500.

2. Minimum lease allowed – 6 months.

3. The lender will use an affordability calculation based on the anticipated rental income.

4. Minimum arrangement fee of £100.

5. Maximum of 3 properties per applicant allowed.

6. Booking fee – £100.

75 per cent LTV

Lender: **Bank of Ireland**

Tel: (0118) 968 4300
Website: www.bank-of-ireland.co.uk

Arrangement fee: Nil
Repayment options: Any
Life insurance required: No
Acceptable areas: England & Wales only

Notes:

1. Minimum valuation of any property – £33,333.
2. Minimum lease allowed – call lender to discuss.
3. DSS, council or student tenants not allowed.
4. A maximum of 5 properties in a portfolio will be allowed. The maximum total lending will be £500,000.
5. The lender calculates the monthly repayment based on 9% and requires the rental income to be 140% of the figure.
6. Minimum age of applicant is 25 and minimum income (outside of rental income) is £15,000.
7. Scheme is Bank of England base rate (currently 4%) plus 1.25% until 1 January 2005, then plus 1.75%.

Lender: **Bank of Scotland**

Tel: (0800) 810 810
Website: www.bankofscotland.co.uk

Arrangement fee: £250.00
Repayment options: Any
Life insurance required: No
Acceptable areas: Available on these terms to customers based in Scotland only. Call above number for details if property is elsewhere in UK.

Notes:

1. Scheme is Bank of England base rate (currently 4%) plus 1.75%.
2. Minimum valuation of any property – £50,000.

3. Maximum of 5 properties per applicant allowed.
4. It is a condition that the applicant's residential mortgage will be held with the bank.
5. Lender will allow up to 5 times the rental income to be taken into account when assessing the loan amount.
6. DSS, council or student tenants not allowed.
7. Minimum arrangement fee – £500.

Lender: **Bath Building Society**

Tel: (01225) 423 271
Website: www.bibs.co.uk
Email: bsoc@bibs.co.uk

Arrangement fee: Nil
Repayment options: Any
Life insurance required: No
Acceptable areas: Will lend only within 50 mile radius of Bath

Notes:

1. Minimum valuation of any property – £40,000.
2. Minimum lease allowed – call lender.
3. DSS or council tenants not allowed.
4. Evidence of income required by a recognised letting agent (ARLA) and must equate to an interest rate of 15%.
5. Rate is lenders Standard Variable Mortgage Rate plus a loading of 1%.

Lender: **Buckinghamshire**

Tel: (01494) 873 064
Website: www.bucksbuildingsociety.com

Arrangement fee: £250.00
Repayment options: Any

Life insurance required: No
Acceptable areas: UK

Notes:

1. Arrangement fee is negotiable – £250 minimum, £500 maximum.

2. No compulsory insurance.

3. Maximum term is 25 years.

4. Purchase or remortgage of residential property which are let subject to an Assured Shorthold Tenancy Agreement.

5. Capital repayments up to 10% allowed each year without penalty.

6. 80% loan to value if advance supported by personal income in addition to rental income.

Lender: **Dunfermline**

Tel: (01383) 627 727
Website: www.dunfermline-bs.co.uk
Email: comments@dunfermline-bs.co.uk

Arrangement fee: £395.00
Repayment options: Any
Life insurance required: No
Acceptable areas: Scotland only

Notes:

1. Minimum valuation of any property – £40,000.

2. Minimum lease allowed – 30 years on maturity of mortgage.

3. DSS, council or student tenants not allowed.

4. Lender has no set criteria – will accept/decline each application on its own merits.

5. Maximum term is 20 years.

6. Maximum 2 properties in addition to main residence.

Lender: **Furness Building Society**

Tel: (0800) 834 312
Website: www.furnessbs.co.uk
Email: call.centre@furness-bs.co.uk

Arrangement fee: £100.00
Repayment options: Any
Life insurance required: No
Acceptable areas: England & Wales

Notes:

1. Maximum term 25 years.

2. Open to UK residents.

3. Borrower must appoint a professional managing agent for the letting.

4. Employed, self-employed and retired borrowers will be considered.

5. 75% of rental income must be sufficient to cover the mortgage payment (not just the interest) at the full rate.

6. Applications cannot be considered where the sole income is derived from rental income.

7. Properties with more than 1 kitchen or more than 5 bedrooms per letting unit will not be accepted.

8. All flats/maisonettes must be purpose-built and self-contained; bedsits not acceptable.

9. Diplomatic, student, housing association and council lets are not considered except where the tenant is a limited company.

10. Maximum number of properties – 15.

Lender: **Harpenden Building Society**

Tel: (01582) 765 411
Website: www.harpendenbs.co.uk
Email: enquiries@harpendenbs.co.uk

Arrangement fee: £200.00
Repayment options: Any
Life insurance required: Yes
Acceptable areas: England only

Notes:

1. Minimum valuation of any property –
    £50,000.
2. DSS, council or student tenants are
    considered.
3. The lender will use an affordability
    calculation based on the anticipated
    rental income.

Lender: **Hinckley & Rugby**

Tel: (01455) 251 234
Website: www.hrbs.co.uk
Email: enquiry@hrbs.co.uk

Arrangement fee: Nil
Repayment options: Any
Life insurance required: Yes
Acceptable areas: East Midlands only

Notes:

1. Minimum valuation of any property –
    £30,000.
2. Minimum lease allowed – 75 years at
    outset of mortgage.
3. DSS, council or student tenants not
    allowed.
4. Rental income less 32.5% – must cover
    the mortgage interest each month.
5. Properties of 4 storeys or more are
    excluded.

6. Rate charged is lenders Standard
    Variable Mortgage Rate (currently
    5.64%) plus a loading of between 1-2%.

Lender: **Leek United Building Society**

Tel: (01538) 392 419
Website: www.leek-united.co.uk

Arrangement fee: £150.00
Repayment options: Any
Life insurance required: No
Acceptable areas: England & Wales

Notes:

1. Minimum valuation of any property –
    £33,333.
2. No DSS, student lets or studio flats.
3. Rental income to be at least 130% more
    than the mortgage interest
    commitment.
4. Gross rental yield to be at least 7%.
5. Lender uses affordability scale
    incorporating income multiples and
    property rental.
6. Can accommodate small portfolios of
    properties.
7. Society will not accept converted
    houses/flats.
8. 1% discount.
9. Loyalty bonus applies after 5 years
    (currently 0.25%).
10. Property to be let on an Assured
    Shorthold Tenancy.

Lender: **Loughborough**

Tel: (01509) 610 600
Website: www.theloughborough.co.uk

Arrangement fee: £250.00
Repayment options: Any

Life insurance required: No
Acceptable areas: East Midlands only

Notes:

1. Portfolio lending allowed.
2. Rental income expected/received must exceed mortgage payment.
3. Rate charged is lenders Standard Variable Mortgage Rate (currently 5.6%) plus a loading of 0.5%.

Lender: **Melton Mowbray**

Tel: (01664) 563 937
Website: www.mmbs.co.uk
Email: melton@mmbs.co.uk

Arrangement fee: £80.00
Repayment options: Capital and Interest
Life insurance required: No
Acceptable areas: 50 mile radius of society's principal office in Leicester

Notes:

1. Maximum of 5 properties per borrower.
2. Maximum total borrowing of £500,000.
3. Multi-occupancy properties are not acceptable.
4. Rental income must cover mortgage payments by a minimum of 130%.
5. An Assured Shorthold Tenancy for a minimum of 6 months and a maximum of 12 months required.

Lender: **Mercantile Building Society**

Tel: (0191) 295 9500
Website: www.mercantile-bs.co.uk
Email: enquiries@mercantile-bs.co.uk

Arrangement fee: £295.00
Repayment options: Any
Life insurance required: No
Acceptable areas: Fully national

Notes:

1. Mortgage secured on properties purchased and let on an Assured Shorthold Tenancy.
2. To qualify, a minimum of 3 properties is required.
3. 1% discount.

Lender: **Monmouthshire**

Tel: (01633) 840 454
Website: www.monbsoc.co.uk

Arrangement fee: £250.00
Repayment options: Any
Life insurance required: No
Acceptable areas: Wales

Notes:

1. Minimum age is 25.
2. No first time buyers.
3. No auction properties or holiday homes.
4. Gross rental must exceed mortgage payment by 30%.
5. Free mortgage payment protection insurance for 6 months, subject to eligibility.
6. Assured Shorthold Tenancy Agreements only.

Lender: **Northern Rock**

Tel: (0845) 605 0500
Website: www.northernrock.co.uk

Arrangement fee: £495.00
Repayment options: Capital and Interest
Life insurance required: No
Acceptable areas: England, Wales &
Scotland allowed

Notes:

1. Minimum valuation of any property –
    £40,000.

2. Up to 4 properties per person.

3. Total exposure – £1 million.

4. Rental income must exceed 100% of
    mortgage repayments.

5. Minimum income must be £25,000 for
    main applicant.

6. Borrower must have an Assured
    Shorthold Tenancy Agreement.

7. Maximum number of applicants – 4.

8. Minimum age is 21.

9. Capital repayments up to 15% allowed
    each year without penalty.

Lender: **Saffron Walden**

Tel: (01799) 522 211
Website: www.swhebs.co.uk

Arrangement fee: £50.00
Repayment options: Any
Life insurance required: Yes
Acceptable areas: Bedfordshire,
Cambridgeshire, Essex, Hertfordshire,
London & Suffolk

Notes:

1. Minimum valuation of any property –
    £13,350.

2. Minimum lease allowed – 50 years on
    maturity of mortgage.

3. Minimum loan for a remortgage is
    £15,100.

4. DSS, council or student tenants not
    allowed.

5. Minimum arrangement fee – £100.
    Lender also charges a completion fee of
    up to 1.5%.

6. Curriculum Vitae and net worth
    statement required on all applicants.

7. Rental income must exceed mortgage
    payments by 75%.

8. Rate is standard variable plus 1%.

Lender: **Stroud & Swindon**

Tel: (0800) 616 112
Website: www.stroudandswindon.co.uk

Arrangement fee: £295.00
Repayment options: Any
Life insurance required: No

Acceptable areas: Fully national

Notes:

1. Minimum valuation of any property –
    £43,000.

2. Minimum lease allowed – 50 years on
    maturity of mortgage.

3. DSS, council or student tenants not
    allowed.

4. Ability to make overpayments and then
    draw on overpayments at a later stage.

5. The lender will use income multiples,
    less existing commitments plus 140% of
    annual rent at 9% to determine
    maximum borrowings.

6. 0.75% discount.

7. Maximum loan of £250,000 per
    property. Total maximum borrowing
    allowed of £500,000 over a portfolio of
    3 properties.

8. No fee remortgage available includes free valuation and legal fees paid if lender's solicitor is used.

Lender: **Sun Bank**

Tel: (01438) 744 555
Website: www.sunbank.co.uk

Arrangement fee: £400.00
Repayment options: Any
Life insurance required: Yes
Acceptable areas: National coverage, although will usually be limited to metropolitan areas

Notes:

1. Minimum valuation – £75,000.
2. Minimum lease allowed – 35 years on maturity of mortgage.
3. 0.8% arrangement fee – minimum £500.
4. Any number of properties, maximum loan limit £1 million.
5. Gross rent must be at least 125% of interest payments.
6. DSS, council or student tenants not allowed.
7. Curriculum Vitae and net worth statement required on all applicants.
8. Property must be subject to an Assured Shorthold Tenancy Agreement.
9. Lender requires all properties to be managed by professional letting agents.
10. Capital repayments of up to 10% allowed each year without penalty.
11. 1.5% discount.

Lender: **Universal Building Society**

Tel: (0191) 232 0973
Website: www.theuniversal.co.uk
Email: enquiries@theuniversal.co.uk

Arrangement fee: £395.00
Repayment options: Any
Life insurance required: Yes
Acceptable areas: North East England only

Notes:

1. Minimum valuation of any property – £40,000.
2. Minimum lease allowed – 35 years on maturity of mortgage.
3. DSS or student tenants are not considered.
4. The lender will use an affordability calculation based on the anticipated rental income.
5. 1% discount.
6. Maximum of 5 properties allowed.

Lender: **Woolwich Direct**

Tel: (0645) 757 575
Website: www.woolwich.co.uk

Arrangement fee: £350.00
Repayment options: Any
Life insurance required: No
Acceptable areas: Fully national

Notes:

1. Minimum lease allowed – 50 years on maturity of mortgage.
2. DSS, council, company or student tenants not considered.
3. The lender will use an affordability calculation based on the anticipated rental income.
4. Gross annual rental income must cover the annual mortgage interest payment by at least 125%.
5. Maximum of 65% for non-UK residents.

6. Base rate tracker (currently 4%) plus 1.2%.

Lender: **Yellow Brick Road**

Tel: (0800) 009 977
Website: www.yellowbrickroad.co.uk

Arrangement fee: £495.00
Repayment options: Any
Life insurance required: No
Acceptable areas: England & Wales

Notes:

1. Rate charged is dependent on applicant's personal circumstances and is based on the LIBOR (see glossary for definition) plus between 3.25% and 5.75%. The applicant's circumstances will also impact on the maximum loan size and the maximum percentage loan (in relation to purchase price or valuation) that is available.

2. Up to 3 months mortgage or rent arrears, no more than 1 month at application.

3. All CCJs count within 3 years of application unless satisfied over 12 months ago.

4. For loans over £200,000 an additional rate of 0.5% will apply.

5. For self-certified loans an additional rate of 0.5% will apply.

6. For remortgages an additional rate of 0.5% will apply.

7. Self-certified remortgage up to 70% LTV and 75% for purchase.

70 per cent LTV

Lender: **Chorley & District**

Tel: (01257) 419 110
Website: www.chorleybs.co.uk
Email: mortgages@chorleybs.co.uk

Arrangement fee: £195.00
Repayment options: Any
Life insurance required: No

Notes:

1. These criteria apply to rental properties within Lancashire.

2. Properties outside Lancashire will be considered on an individual basis.

3. Rental income must exceed 120% of mortgage repayments.

4. Full status only.

5. 6-month Shorthold Tenancy Agreement is mandatory, maximum term for same is 12 months.

6. Housing associations or companies cannot be parties to the tenancy agreement.

7. Multiple Tenancy Agreements are not acceptable on 1 property.

8. DSS, council or student tenants not allowed nor properties divided into bedsits.

Lender: **NatWest**

Tel: (0345) 023 845
Website: www.natwest.co.uk
Email: nwmsbtl@natwest.com

Arrangement fee: £200.00
Repayment options: Capital and Interest
Life insurance required: Yes
Acceptable areas: National coverage

Notes:

1. Minimum valuation of any property – £20,000.

2. Minimum lease allowed – 35 years on maturity of mortgage.

3. Maximum of 4 properties per applicant.

4. DSS, council or student tenants not allowed.

5. Lender uses standard income multiples of 3 times main income, plus one times the rental income less commitments. Also rental income must be 130% of mortgage payment.

6. Minimum joint income required of £20,000.

7. 1.7% discount.

60 per cent LTV

Lender: **Market Harborough**

Tel: (01858) 463 244
Website: www.mhbs.co.uk
Email: CustomersFirst@mhbs.co.uk

Arrangement fee: £295.00
Repayment options: Any
Life insurance required: Yes
Acceptable areas: England, Scotland & Wales

Notes:

1. Minimum valuation of any property – £40,000.

2. Minimum lease allowed – 50 years on maturity of mortgage.

3. Lender charges additional £50 booking fee.

4. DSS, council or student tenants not allowed.

5. 1% discount.

6. Maximum of 3 properties allowed.

7. Capital repayments up to 10% allowed each year without penalty.

8. 6-month Assured Shorthold Tenancy Agreements only.

50 per cent LTV

Lender: **Standard Life Bank**

Tel: (0845) 609 0262
Website: www.standardlifebank.com
Email: slb_mortgages@standardlife.com

Arrangement fee: £350.00
Repayment options: Any
Life insurance required: No
Acceptable areas: UK

Notes:

1. Minimum age of applicant is 25 years, maximum age is 60 years.

2. Minimum employment income – £20,000 single or £30,000 joint excluding rental income.

3. Maximum total loans – £500,000 (maximum £400,000 for a single property).

4. Up to 5 rental properties.

5. Overpayments allowed (£1,000 minimum lump sums).

6. Up to 2 payment holidays allowed per year per property.

7. Lender charges interest on a daily basis.

8. Annual rental income must equal at least 10% of the loan amount.

9. 1% discount.

iii) List of property websites

The list of websites broken down by region below enables you to search for properties in the area that interests you. All these sites direct you ultimately to the estate agent that is selling the property. There are also rental sites included in this list, so you can keep abreast of the current market rental values of properties you have or are currently interested in.

I personally use rightmove.co.uk, ukpropertyshop.com and home.co.uk to find my properties. These sites seem professionally run and have a large database of properties for sale.

I would suggest you search for properties listed in the hotspots detailed in part vi) of this chapter.

Sales and rental websites

1. www.accommodatingcompany.co.uk
2. www.accommodation.com
3. www.accommodation-directory.co.uk
4. www.ashtons.co.uk
5. www.asserta.co.uk
6. www.bainprop.co.uk
7. www.bansalestates.co.uk
8. www.cdproperty.co.uk
9. www.claridges-estates.co.uk
10. www.coppingjoyce.co.uk
11. www.dauntons.co.uk
12. www.davisestates.co.uk
13. www.fish4homes.co.uk
14. www.forgetestateagents.co.uk
15. www.foxtons.co.uk
16. www.froglet.com
17. www.halfapercent.com
18. www.haylingproperty.co.uk
19. www.home.co.uk
20. www.homesdujour.com
21. www.home-sale.co.uk
22. www.housedeals.co.uk
23. www.housesearchuk.co.uk
24. www.londonpropertyguide.co.uk
25. www.londonshome.co.uk
26. www.lookproperty.co.uk
27. www.milburys.co.uk
28. www.mondial-property.co.uk
29. www.national-property-register.co.uk
30. www.nicholasirwin.co.uk
31. www.numberone4property.co.uk
32. www.palmsagency.co.uk
33. www.primelocation.com
34. www.propertyadsonline.co.uk
35. www.propertyfinder.co.uk
36. www.propertylive.co.uk
37. www.propertymatters.co.uk

38. www.p4L.co.uk

39. www.rentalsandsales.co.uk

40. www.rightmove.co.uk

41. www.sequencehome.co.uk

42. www.shobrook.co.uk

43. www.stonegateestates.co.uk

44. www.themovechannel.com

45. www.ukpropertyguide.co.uk

46. www.underoneroof.com

47. www.vebra.com

Sales only websites

1. www.agentfreesales.co.uk

2. www.andrewpontin.co.uk

3. www.assertahome.com

4. www.bennettjones.co.uk

5. www.capital-residence.co.uk

6. www.daltons.co.uk

7. www.dmea.co.uk

8. www.estate-agent-property.co.uk

9. www.fairview.co.uk

10. www.gatehouseestates.co.uk

11. www.globalmart.co.uk

12. www.hamiltonbrooks.co.uk

13. www.homehunter.co.uk

14. www.homepages.co.uk

15. www.homesalez.com

16. www.homeselluk.com

17. www.homes-uk.co.uk

18. www.hotproperty.co.uk

19. www.housemarket.co.uk

20. www.housenet.co.uk

21. www.houseweb.co.uk

22. www.howards.co.uk

23. www.jparissteele.co.uk

24. www.lakewood-properties.co.uk

25. www.michaeltucker.co.uk

26. www.newey.co.uk

27. www.newhomesnetwork.co.uk

28. www.owner-property-sales.co.uk

29. www.paramount-properties.co.uk

30. www.partake.co.uk

31. www.pickits.co.uk

32. www.pro-net.co.uk

33. www.properties-direct.com

34. www.propertyfinderwales.co.uk

35. www.propertysales.co.uk

36. www.propertyworld.com

37. www.property-go.co.uk

38. www.property4uk.co.uk

39. www.reale-state.co.uk

40. www.smartestates.com

41. www.smartnewhomes.com

42. www.stewartwatson.co.uk

43. www.thehousehunter.co.uk

44. www.thelondonoffice.co.uk

45. www.tspc.co.uk

46. www.ukpropertysales.net

47. www.ukpropertyshop.co.uk

48. www.uk-property.com

49. www.uk-property-sale-directory.co.uk

50. www.villagategroup.com

51. www.walsall-estates.co.uk

52. www.wisemove.co.uk

53. www.your-life.co.uk

54. www.your-move.co.uk

Rentals only

1. www.assuredproprentals.co.uk

2. www.cambridge-rentals.co.uk

3. www.chester.com/propertyrentals

4. www.citylets.co.uk

5. www.excel-property.co.uk

6. www.faulknerproperty.co.uk

7. www.flemingpropertyrentals.co.uk

8. www.homelet.co.uk

9. www.letonthenet.com

10. www.letsrentuk.com

11. www.letters.co.uk

12. www.lettingweb.com

13. www.mossoak.co.uk

14. www.net-lettings.co.uk

15. www.palacegate.co.uk

16. www.property-go.co.uk

17. www.simplyrent.co.uk

18. www.spacetorent.com

19. www.studenthousehunt.com

20. www.studentpad.co.uk

21. www.sunkissed.co.uk

22. www.torent.co.uk

iv) Mortgage brokers

A local mortgage broker can be found quite easily through the Yellow Pages or www.yell.com. You can use my mortgage broker if you wish. Her name is Liz Syms and she can be contacted on Tel: (01708) 443 334; Fax: (01708) 470 043. If you mention the reference 'Ajay Ahuja', you will receive a discount on her fees of up to 50 per cent. She is very good – this is why I use her! If not, I suggest you go for a buy-to-let specialist mortgage broker. These can be found from the following websites. You have to specify a buy-to-let specialist when searching:

www.ifap.org.uk & www.unbiased.co.uk

IFA Promotion Ltd, 2nd Floor, 117 Farringdon Road, London, EC1R 3BX.

Tel: (0800) 085 3250

www.ifawindow.co.uk

Web-based only.

www.searchifa.co.uk

Unit 9, Alpha Business Park, Travellers Close, Hatfield, AL9 7NT.

Tel: (01707) 251 111
Fax: (01707) 272 470
Email: ifa-info@searchifa.co.uk

v) List of accommodation projects

Accommodation projects can find tenants, guarantee and collect the rent and liaise with the tenants on your behalf. Basically, they can act like an agent for you but the great thing is that they provide their service for FREE! The reason they can provide this service for free is because they are non-profit organisations or charities. Consequently, it would be beneficial to donate to the project you use intermittently in order to encourage good relations.

England

1. Accommodation Bonds for Cornwall, Stonham Housing with Care, PO Box 113, Redruth, Cornwall, TR15 2YP.

    Tel: (01209) 216 166
    Website: www.stonhamhousing.org.uk

2. Accommodation Concern, 15 London Road, Kettering, Northants, NN16 0EF.

    Tel: (01536) 416 560
    Website: www.kettering.gov.uk

3. Accommodation DIGS (Cumbria), Housing Strategy Group, South

Lakeland House, Lowther Street, Kendal, Cumbria, LA9 4UD.

Tel: (01539) 733 333
Website: www.southlakeland.gov.uk

4. Alone In London Magnet Project, 188 Kings Cross Road, London, WC1X 9DE.

    Tel: (020) 7278 4224

5. Ashford Borough Council, Civic Centre, Tannery Lane, Ashford, Kent, TN23 1PL.

    Tel: (01233) 330 419
    Website: www.ashford.gov.uk
    Email: enquiries@ashford.gov.uk

6. Banbury Homes Rent Deposit Scheme, 1 Mawle Court, George Street, Banbury, Oxfordshire, OX16 5BP.

    Tel: (01295) 265 439

7. Barnet Housing Aid Centre Rent Deposit Scheme, 36B Woodhouse Road, North Finchley, London, N12 0RG.

    Tel: (020) 8446 2504

8. Basildon Community Resource Centre, 1 The Gore, Basildon, Essex, SS14 2EA.

    Tel: (01268) 450 041

9. Bedfordshire Housing Aid Centre, 68 Tavistock Street, Bedford, Bedfordshire, MK40 2RG.

    Tel: (01234) 328 488

10. Birmingham Bond Scheme Ltd,
    191 Corporation Street,
    Birmingham, B4 6RP.

    Tel: (0121) 233 0257

11. Bolton Bond Board, 5 Great Moor
    Street, Bolton, Lancashire,
    BL1 1NZ.

    Tel: (01204) 366 328

12. Boston Accommodation Bureau,
    14-16 High Street, Lincolnshire,
    PE21 8SH.

    Tel: (01205) 359 664
    Website: www.boston.gov.uk

13. Bournemouth Churches Housing
    Association Rent Deposit Scheme,
    St. Swithun's House, 21
    Christchurch Road, Bournemouth,
    Dorset,
    BH1 3NS.

    Tel: (01202) 410 500

14. Brent Council Rent Deposit
    Guarantee Scheme, Private Housing
    Information Unit, Quality House,
    249 Willesden Lane, Willesden,
    London, NW2 5JH.

    Tel: (020) 8937 2777
    Website: www.brent.gov.uk

15. Brentwood Housing Trust Ltd,
    The Lodge, 28 St. Thomas Road,
    Brentwood, Essex, CM14 4DB.

    Tel: (01277) 225 084

16. Bridge Housing Association,
    33-35 Jamestown Road, Camden,
    London, NW1 7DB.

Tel: (020) 7267 0070

17. Bristol Deposit Guarantee Scheme,
    Conygre House, Conygre Road,
    Filton, South Glos, BS34 7DD.

    Tel: (01454) 865 548
    Website: www.southglos.gov.uk

18. CAN Homeless Action Team, PO
    Box 5164, The Maple Centre,
    Northampton, NN1 3ZP.

    Tel: (01604) 250 678

19. Cannock Chase Churches Housing
    Coalition, Housing & Health Advice
    Centre, 29-31 Park Road, Cannock,
    Staffordshire, WS11 1JN.

    Tel: (01543) 577 572
    Website: www.chasehousing.co.uk
    Email: advicecentre@cannock
    chasedc.gov.uk

20. Charnwood Shelter Project,
    The Annex, Southfield Road,
    Loughborough, Leicestershire,
    LE11 2TS.

    Tel: (01509) 260 500
    Website: www.charnwoodshelter.
    org.uk
    Email: contact@charnwoodshelter.
    org.uk

21. Chelmsford Borough Council,
    Housing Advice & Welfare Rights,
    Civic Centre, Coval Lane,
    Chelmsford, Essex, CM1 1JE.

    Tel: (01245) 606 606
    Website: www.chelmsfordbc.gov.uk
    Email: housing@chelmsfordbc.gov.uk

22. Cheltenham Bond Scheme,
Cheltenham Housing Aid Centre,
31 Prestbury Road, Cheltenham,
Gloucestershire, GL52 2PP.

    Tel: (01242) 226 672
    Website: www.chac.org.uk
    Email: Chelthousingaid@aol.com

23. Chesterfield Borough Council
Deposit Guarantee Scheme, Town
Hall, Rose Hill, Chesterfield,
Derbyshire, S40 1LP.

    Tel: (01246) 345 143
    Website: www.chesterfieldbc.gov.uk

24. Christian Action & Resource
Enterprise, 257-259 Freeman Street,
Grimsby, North East Lincolnshire,
DN37 9DW.

    Tel: (01472) 232 309

25. Churches Acting Together,
191 Park View, Whitley Bay,
Tyne & Wear, NE26 3RD.

    Tel: (0191) 251 4014

26. Churches Housing Action Team,
44 Westexe South, Tiverton, Devon,
EX16 5DH.

    Tel: (01884) 255 606

27. Churches National Housing
Coalition, Housing Justice, Central
Buildings, Oldham Street,
Manchester, M1 1JT.

    Tel: (0161) 236 9321
    Website: www.justhousing.org.uk
    Email: coalition@justhousing.co.uk

28. City Centre Project, YMCA
Building, Trinity Road, Bradford,
West Yorkshire, BD5 0JG.

    Tel: (01274) 736 507

29. Colchester Borough Council,
Housing Advice, PO Box 884, Town
Hall, Colchester, Essex, CO1 1FR.

    Tel: (01206) 282 555
    Website: www.colchester.gov.uk

30. Craven Housing Scheme,
28 Victoria Street, Skipton,
North Yorkshire, BD23 1JE.

    Tel: (01756) 701 110

31. Croydon Churches Housing
Association Ltd, Rent in Advance
Scheme, 92 Church Road, Croydon,
Surrey, CR0 1SD.

    Tel: (020) 8688 2845

32. Croydon Home Bond, Look Ahead
Housing and Care, 282-284
Brigstock Road, Thornton Heath,
Surrey, CR7 7JE.

    Tel: (020) 8689 9559

33. Dacorum Borough Council, HAC,
138 The Marlowes, Hemel
Hempstead, Hertfordshire,
HP1 1EZ.

    Tel: (01442) 228 900
    Website: www.dacorum.gov.uk

34. Dacorum Rent Aid,
23A High Street, Hemel Hempstead,
Hertfordshire, HP1 3AA.

Tel: (01442) 251213
Website: www.dacorumrentaid.org
Email: dacorum.rentaid@
btopenworld.com

35. Darlington Bond & Rent Guarantee
Scheme, The Baptist Church,
Grange Road, Darlington,
Co Durham, DL1 5NH.

Tel: (01325) 467 617
Website: www.darlingtoncharity.
fsnet.co.uk
Email: bondscheme@darlington
charity.fsnet.co.uk

36. Derby Bond Bank Scheme, Housing
Options Centre, Bio House,
Derwent Street, Derby, DE1 2ED.

Tel: (01332) 716 483
Email: housing.options@derby.gov.uk

37. Detached Youth Work Project,
50 Piccadilly, York, North Yorkshire,
YO1 9NX.

Tel: (01904) 651 431

38. Dudley MBC Guaranteed Rent
Deposit Scheme (Stourbridge
District), Private Sector Housing,
17 St. James's Road, Dudley, West
Midlands, DY1 1JG.

Tel: (01384) 814 313
Website: www.dudley.gov.uk

39. Elmbridge Rentstart, CAB Offices,
Harry Fletcher House, High Street,
Esher, Surrey, KT10 9RN.

Tel: (01372) 477 167
Email: elmbridge_rentstart@yahoo.
co.uk

40. Epsom & Ewell Borough Council,
Community Housing Project, Town
Hall, The Parade, Epsom, Surrey,
KT18 5BY.

Tel: (01372) 732 437
Website: www.epsom-ewell.gov.uk

41. Equity Trust Fund, Room 222
Africa House, 64-78 Kingsway,
London, WC2B 6AH.

Tel: (020) 7404 6041

42. Face-To-Face, 14 St David's Road
South, Lytham St Anne's,
Lancashire, FY8 1TB.

Tel: (01253) 720 270

43. Fareport Fund-A-Home,
X-perience, Trinity Street, Fareham,
Hampshire, PO16 7SJ.

Tel: (01329) 230 234

44. Foundation Housing, Tennant Hall,
Blenheim Grove, Leeds, West
Yorkshire, LS2 9ET.

Tel: (0113) 368 8800
Website: www.foundationhousing.
org.uk
Email: cst@foundationhousing.org.uk

45. Greater Manchester RDS
(Rochdale), Grants & Enforcements
Department, Municipal Offices,
Smith Street, Rochdale, Lancashire,
OL16 1LQ.

Tel: (01706) 866 680
Website: www.rochdale.gov.uk

46. Greenwich Deposit Guarantee
Scheme, London Borough of

Greenwich, Housing Aid Centre, 125 Powis Street, Woolwich, SE18 6JL.

Tel: (020) 8854 8888
Website: www.greenwich.gov.uk
Email: Housingaidcentre@ greenwich.gov.uk

47. Guaranteed Accommodation Payments Scheme, YMCA, Peartree Lane, Welwyn Garden City, Hertfordshire, AL7 3UL.

    Tel: (01707) 351 400

48. Harlow Accommodation Project, 2A Wych Elm, Harlow, Essex, CM20 1QP.

    Tel: (01279) 861 186
    Website: www.harlow.gov.uk

49. Hastings & Rother Bond Board, 49 Cambridge Gardens, Hastings, East Sussex, TN34 1EN.

    Tel: (01424) 721 775

50. Help The Homeless (Chorley), 45 Clifford Street, Chorley, Lancashire, PR7 1SE.

    Tel: (01257) 273 320

51. Herefordshire Council Deposit Guarantee Scheme, Housing Services Division, Garrick House, Widemarsh Street, Hereford, HR4 9EU.

    Tel: (01432) 261 580
    Website: www.herefordshire.gov.uk

52. HMP The Mount, 1 Molyneaux Avenue, Bovington, Hertfordshire, HP3 0NZ.

    Tel: (01442) 834 363

53. Homeless in Oswestry Action Partnership, Centre North West, Oak Street, Oswestry, Shropshire, SY11 1LW.

    Tel: (01691) 650 850
    Website: www.hoap.org.uk

54. Homelink, 45-47 Blythe Street, London, E2 6LN.

    Tel: (020) 7729 7573
    Email: homelink@dial.pipex.com

55. Housing Young People in Shrewsbury, Suite H, Roy Fletcher Centre, 12-17 Cross Hill, Shrewsbury, Shropshire, SY1 1JE.

    Tel: (01743) 341 900

56. Huntingdonshire District Council Rent Deposit Scheme, Pathfinder House, St Mary's Street, Huntingdon, Cambridgeshire, PE29 3TN.

    Tel: (01480) 388 230
    Website: www.huntingdonshire. gov.uk

57. Isle of Wight Deposit Guarantee Scheme, Exchange House, St Cross Lane, Newport, Isle of Wight, PO30 5BZ.

    Tel: (01983) 524 715

58. Key House Project, 130 North Street, Keighley, West Yorkshire, BD21 3AD.

    Tel: (01535) 211 311

59. Kingston Churches Action on Homelessness, The Access Project, 36a Fife Road, Kingston Upon Thames, Surrey, KT1 1SU.

    Tel: (020) 8255 2439
    Website: www.kcah.org.uk
    Email: info@kcah.org.uk

60. Kirklees Bond Bank, 1st Floor, Standard House, Half Moon Street, Huddersfield, West Yorkshire, HD1 2JF.

    Tel: (01484) 223 922

61. Lancashire Housing Aid Centre, 35A-C North Albert Street, Fleetwood, Lancashire, FY7 6AJ.

    Tel: (01253) 874 324

62. Leicester City Council, Housing Advice Centre, Alliance House, 6 Bishop Street, Leicester, LE1 6AF.

    Tel: (0116) 222 2699
    Website: www.leicester.gov.uk

63. Lewes District Churches Homelink, Lewes District Council, Lewes House, 32 High Street, Lewes, East Sussex, BN7 2LX.

    Tel: (01273) 471 600
    Website: www.lewes.gov.uk

64. Lifeshare Resettlement Service, 23 New Mount Street, Manchester, M4 4DE.

    Tel: (0161) 953 4069
    Website: www.lifeshare.co.uk
    Email: office@lifeshare.co.uk

65. Littlehampton Churches Together Homelink, Room 1, Arcade Chambers, 86 High Street, Littlehampton, West Sussex, BN17 5DX.

    Tel: (01903) 739 699

66. London Borough Barnet Private Sector Tenancy Scheme, 1st Floor, Barnet House, 1255 High Road, London, N20 0EJ.

    Tel: (020) 8359 4863
    Website: www.barnet.gov.uk

67. London Borough Sutton Housing Centre, Civic Offices, St Nicholas Way, Sutton, Surrey, SM1 1EA.

    Tel: (020) 8770 5800
    Website: www.sutton.gov.uk

68. Malvern Hills District Council, Housing Recreation & Community Services, Highlea, 36 Church Street, Malvern, Worcestershire, WR14 2AZ.

    Tel: (01684) 862 181
    Website: www.malvernhills.gov.uk

69. Mendip District Council Rent Guarantee Scheme, YMCA, The Old Glasshouse, South Street, Wells, Somerset, BA5 1SL.

    Tel: (01749) 670 761

70.   NACRO Resettlement Services,
      169 Clapham Road, London,
      SW9 0PU.

      Tel: (020) 7582 6500
      Website: www.nacro.org.uk

71.   Newark & Sherwood District
      Council, Kelham Hall, Kelham,
      Newark, Nottinghamshire,
      NG23 5QX.

      Tel: (01636) 650 000
      Website: www.newark-sherwooddc.
      gov.uk

72.   No. 5 Youth Counselling and
      Information, 2-4 Sackville Street,
      Reading, Berkshire, RG1 1NT.

      Tel: (0118) 901 5652
      Website: www.no5.org.uk
      Email: housing@no5.org.uk

73.   North Herts Homeless Development
      Team, Footings/
      Deposit Guarantee Scheme, 25 Sun
      Street, Hitchin, Hertfordshire,
      SG5 1AH.

      Tel: (01462) 435 668

74.   North Manchester Bond Scheme,
      c/o Family Housing Association,
      206 Lightbowrne Road, Manchester,
      M40 5EE.

      Tel: (0161) 682 1500

75.   North Wilts District Council Rent
      Deposit Guarantee Scheme,
      Monkton Park, Chippenham,
      Wiltshire SN15 1ER.

      Tel: (01249) 706 111
      Website: www.northwilts.gov.uk
      Email: housing@northwilts.gov.uk

76.   Northampton Borough Council,
      Housing & Money Advice Centre,
      Fish Street, Northampton,
      NN1 2AA.

      Tel: (01604) 838 700
      Website: www.northampton.gov.uk

77.   Nugent Care Society, 99 Edge Lane,
      Edge Hill, Liverpool, L7 2PE.

      Tel: (0151) 261 2000
      Website: www.nugentcare.org
      Email: info@nugentcare.org

78.   Oldham Independent Housing Aid
      Centre, 5 Ashcroft Court, Peter
      Street, Oldham, Lancashire,
      OL1 1HP.

      Tel: (0161) 624 0674

79.   Open Door Deposit Scheme, Shelter
      Housing Aid Centre, The Food
      Centre, 793 Avebury Boulevard,
      Milton Keynes, Bedfordshire,
      MK9 3NW.

      Tel: (01908) 667 599
      Email: info@odoor.fsnet.co.uk

80.   Oxford Citizens Housing
      Association, Deposit Guarantee
      Scheme, 244 Barns Road, Oxford,
      OK4 3RW.

      Tel: (01865) 773 000

81.   Plymouth Access To Housing, The
      Harwell Centre, 28-42 Harwell
      Court, Western Approach, Plymouth,
      Devon, PL1 1PY.

Tel: (01752) 223 823

82. Preston YMCA, Samuel Street,
Preston, Lancashire, PR1 4YE.

Tel: (01772) 794 103

83. Project 2041, 3 Ashley Court, High
Street, Yiewsley, Middlesex,
UB7 7DN.

Tel: (01895) 462 073
Website: www.project2041.org.uk
Email: enquiries@project2041.
org.uk

84. Reading Borough Council Rent
Deposit Scheme, Housing Advice
Centre, Civic Centre, Reading,
Berkshire, RG1 7TD.

Tel: (0118) 939 0089
Website: www.reading.gov.uk

85. Reigate & Redhill YMCA Rent
Deposit Scheme, Princes Road,
Redhill, Surrey, RH1 6JJ.

Tel: (01737) 779 979

86. Robond, Room 7, The Guardian
Centre, Drummond Street,
Rotherham, South Yorkshire,
S65 1HX.

Tel: (01709) 828 791
Email: staff.robond@virgin.net

87. Room4u, Private Sector Team
Housing Group, Town Hall,
Watford, WD17 3EX.

Tel: (01923) 278 145

88. Runnymede Rentstart,
12-13 The Sainsbury Centre,
Chertsey, Surrey, KT16 9AG.

Tel: (01932) 567 621
Email: runnymede.rentstart@tiscali.
co.uk

89. Ryedale Bond Guarantee Scheme,
Ryedale House, Malton, North
Yorkshire, YO17 7HH.

Tel: (01653) 600 666
Website: www.ryedale.gov.uk

90. St Helen's Metropolitan Borough
Council, Housing Advice Centre,
Ground Floor, Wesley House,
Corporation Street, St Helen's,
Merseyside, WA10 1HE.

Tel: (01744) 456 329

91. Sarsen Housing Association, Sarsen
Court, Horton Avenue, Cannings
Hill, Devizes, Wiltshire, SN10 2AZ.

Tel: (01380) 720 027
Website: www.sarsen.co.uk
Email: sarsen@sarsen.co.uk

92. Sevenoaks District Council Private
Letting Scheme, Community
Services, Council Offices, Argyle
Road, Sevenoaks, Kent, TN13 1HG.

Tel: (01732) 227 000
Website: www.sevenoaks.gov.uk

93. Shrewsbury Homes for All, Suite H,
Roy Fletcher Centre, 12-17 Cross
Hill, Shrewsbury, Shropshire,
SY1 1JE.

Tel: (01743) 231 415

94. SmartMove (Action on Homelessness W Wilts), 12-13 Duke Street, Trowbridge, Wiltshire, BA14 8EA.

    Tel: (01225) 719 045

95. SmartMove (Barnsley), English Churches Housing, 1st Floor, Wellington House, 36 Wellington Street, Barnsley S70 1WA.

    Tel: (01226) 785 893

96. SmartMove (Calderdale), 9 Portland Place, Halifax, HX1 2JQ.

    Tel: (01422) 361 515
    Email: calderdale.smartmove@virgin.net

97. SmartMove (CRISIS), 64 Commercial Street, London, E1 6LT.

    Tel: (0870) 011 3335

98. SmartMove (Exeter Homeless Action Group), 16 Bartholomew Street East, Exeter, Devon, EX4 3BG.

    Tel: (01392) 430 228

99. SmartMove (Great Yarmouth), Bauleah House, 51 St Nicholas Road, Great Yarmouth, Norfolk, NR30 1NR.

    Tel: (01493) 331 524
    Email: smartmove.gy@virgin.net

100. SmartMove (Grenfell Housing Association),16th Floor, The Tower, 125 High Street, Colliers Wood, London, SW19 2JG.

    Tel: (020) 8545 2588
    Email: info@grenfell-housing.co.uk

101. SmartMove (Hartlepool), Housing Advice and Tenancy Support, Hartlepool Citizens Advice Bureau, 87 Park Road, Hartlepool, TS26 9HP.

    Tel: (01429) 277 030
    Email: team@htss.fsnet.co.uk

102. SmartMove (Hull Hostel Forum), Hull YPI, 83-93 George Street, Hull, HU1 3BN.

    Tel: (01482) 620 360
    Email: hullhostelforum@care4free.ne

103. SmartMove (M25 Group), 46 Netherhall Road, Doncaster, DN1 2PZ.

    Tel: (01302) 327 499

104. SmartMove (NOMAD), 30 Rockingham Lane, Sheffield, South Yorkshire, S1 4FW.

    Tel: (0114) 273 8805
    Email: NomadSmartMove@aol.com

105. SmartMove (North Cornwall), St Petrocs Society, 8 City Road, Truro, Cornwall, TR1 2JJ.

    Tel: (01872) 264 153
    Website: www.stpetrocs.org.uk
    Email: home@stpetrocs.org.uk

106. SmartMove (Nottingham), 21 Clarendon Street, Nottingham, NG1 5HR.

    Tel: (0115) 859 9500
    Email: smartmove@hlg.org.uk

107. SmartMove (Southport and Sefton), Southport Housing Centre, 68 Eastbank Street, Southport, PR8 1ES.

    Tel: (01704) 501 256

108. SmartMove (Teesside) Rent Bond Guarantee Scheme, Advice & Information Centre, Bath Lane, Stockton-on-Tees, Cleveland, TS18 2EQ.

    Tel: (01642) 351 255
    Email: stocksmart@ukonline.co.uk

109. South Gloucestershire Bond Scheme, 23 The Parade, Coniston Road, Patchway, Bristol, BS34 5LP.

    Tel: (01454) 865 742

110. South Gloucestershire Council, Conygre House, Conygre Road, Filton, Bristol, BS34 7DD.

    Tel: (01454) 865 450
    Website: www.southglos.gov.uk
    Email: Housing@southglos.gov.uk

111. South Holland Housing Aid, Council Offices, Priory Road, Spalding, Lincs, PE11 2XE.

    Tel: (01775) 761 161

112. South Ribble Rent Guarantee Scheme, Civic Centre, West Paddock, Leyland, Preston, Lancashire, PR5 1DH.

    Tel: (01772) 625 371/374

113. South Shropshire Young Persons Housing Project, Marston Mill, Portcullis Lane, Ludlow, Shropshire, SY8 1PZ.

    Tel: (01584) 877 335
    Website: www.ssyphp.net
    Email: ssyphp@care4free.net

114. South Somerset Accommodation Scheme, Morley House, West Hendford, Yeovil, Somerset, BA20 1XE.

    Tel: (01935) 433 008
    Website: www.somerset.gov.uk

115. Southampton City Council Deposit Guarantee Scheme, Housing Advice Centre, Southbrook Rise, 4-8 Millbrook Road East, Southampton, Hampshire, SO15 1YG.

    Tel: (023) 8083 2735
    Website: www.southampton.gov.uk

116. Spelthorne Rentstart Ltd, The Community Link Centre, Knowle Green, Staines, Middlesex, TW18 1XB.

    Tel: (01784) 446 422

117. Stroud District Council, Directorate of Housing & Environmental Services, Ebley Mill, Westward Road, Ebley, Stroud, GL5 4UB.

    Tel: (01453) 754 078
    Website: www.stroud.gov.uk

118. Tameside Rent Deposit Scheme, Wellington Road, Ashton-under-Lyne, OL6 6DL.

    Tel: (0161) 343 7230
    Website: www.tameside.gov.uk/tmbc/rentdeposit.htm

Email: rentdeposit@mail.tameside.gov.uk

119. Tandridge Rent Deposit Scheme, 14 Gresham Road, Oxted, Surrey, RH8 0BQ.

    Tel: (01883) 715 785

120. THATCH, c/o 10 Nicola Close, Harrow Weald, Harrow, Middlesex, HA3 5HP.

    Tel: (020) 8864 0004

121. The Bridge Accommodation Project, 50 Duck Street, Rushden, Northamptonshire, NN10 9SD.

    Tel: (01933) 419 399

122. The Clockwise Centre, 85-87 Pier Avenue, Clacton-on-Sea, Essex, CO15 1QE.

    Tel: (01255) 423 466

123. Three Rivers District Council, Housing Needs & Resources, Three Rivers House, Northway, Rickmansworth, Hertfordshire, WD3 1RL.

    Tel: (01923) 776 611
    Website: www.threerivers.gov.uk
    Email: enquiries@threerivers.gov.uk

124. Threshold Centre Ltd, 4th Floor, Bedford House, 215 Balham High Road, London, SW17 7BQ.

    Tel: (020) 8749 2925

125. Thurrock Deposit Guarantee Scheme, c/o Open Door,

24-28 Orsett Road, Grays, Essex, RM17 5EB.

    Tel: (01375) 396 038

126. Trafford Rent Guarantee Scheme, Housing Options, Urmston Council Offices, Croftsbank Road, Urmston, M41 0UD.

    Tel: (0161) 912 2745
    Website: www.trafford.gov.uk

127. Two Saints Ltd (Society of St Dismas), 30 Cranbury Avenue, Southampton, Hampshire, SO14 0LT.

    Tel: (023) 8022 7933
    Email: info@homelesspages.co.uk

128. Two Step, 163-165 Tooting High Street, Tooting, London, SW17 0SY.

    Tel: (020) 8672 0100

129. Vale of White Horse District Council, Revenues & Benefits Department, Abbey House, Abingdon, Oxon, OX14 3JE.

    Tel: (01235) 520 202
    Website: www.whitehorsedc.gov.uk

130. Voluntary Hostels Group, Wensum House, 10A Wensum Street, Norwich, Norfolk, NR3 1HR.

    Tel: (01603) 617 299
    Website: www.vhg-east.org

131. Wakefield Rent Deposit Scheme, 4-5 The Springs, Wakefield, West Yorkshire, WF1 1PU.

Tel: (01924) 302 085
Website: www.wakefield.gov.uk
Email: HSG-HousingAid@
wakefield.gov.uk

132. Walsall Rent Guarantee Scheme,
PO Box 1427, Walsall, West
Midlands, WS4 2YT.

Tel: (01922) 746 798

133. Waltham Forest Community Based
Housing Association, 433-443 High
Road, Leytonstone, London,
E11 4JU.

Tel: (020) 8988 7500

134. Warrington Borough Council Rent
Deposit Scheme, Housing Services
Department, Bank House, 88
Sankey Street, Warrington, Cheshire,
WA1 1RH.

Tel: (01925) 442 448

135. Waveney District Council Rent
Deposit Guarantee Scheme,
Housing Department, 80 Clapham
Road South, Lowestoft, Suffolk,
NR32 1RB.

Tel: (01502) 523 141

136. West Wiltshire Accommodation
Project, c/o West Wiltshire Housing
Society, Bryer Ash Business Park,
Bradford Road, Trowbridge,
Wiltshire, BA14 8RT.

Tel: (01225) 715 715

137. Winchester Rent Guarantee
Scheme, c/o Feriends Meeting Hall,
Colebrook Street, Winchester,
Hampshire, SO23 9LR.

Tel: (01962) 862 681

138. Wintercomfort Rent Deposit
Scheme, Overstream House, Victoria
Avenue, Cambridge, CB4 1EG.

Tel: (01223) 518 140

139. Woking Association for the Single
Homeless, Woking Churches Rent
Guarantee Scheme, Pound House,
35-47 Board School Road, Woking,
Surrey, GU21 5HD.

Tel: (01483) 720 872

140. Woodspring Deposit Guarantee
Board, Room 9, YMCA, 2 Bristol
Road Lower, Weston Super Mare,
Somerset, BS23 2PN.

Tel: (01934) 629 787

141. Worcester Welfare Rights Centre,
Angel Centre, Angel Place, Worcester,
WR1 3QN.

Tel: (01905) 612 774

142. Wycombe Rent Deposit Guarantee
Scheme, 52 Frogmoor, High
Wycombe, Buckinghamshire,
HP13 5DG.

Tel: (01494) 528 557

143. Young Homeless Project Rent
Deposit Guarantee Scheme,
38-38A High Street, Leamington
Spa, Warwickshire, CV31 1LW.

Tel: (01926) 883 179

Northern Ireland

144. Cookstown and Western Shores Area Network, Rural Supported Housing Programme, The Crieve Centre, 2 Hillhead, Stewartstown, Co. Tyrone, BT71 5HY.

    Tel: (028) 773 8845
    Website: www.cookstownwestern shores.com
    Email: cwsan@aol.com

145. Council for the Homeless Northern Ireland, 72 North Street, Belfast, BT1 1LD.

    Tel: (028) 9024 6440
    Website: www.chni.org.uk
    Email: info@chni.org.uk

146. Foyle Homeless Action and Advice Service, SmartMove Rent Deposit Scheme, 28A Bishop Street, Londonderry, BT48 6PP.

    Tel: (028) 7126 6115
    Website: www.first-housing.com
    Email: info@first-housing.com

Republic of Ireland

147. Simon Freshstart, Dublin Simon Community, Dermott Street, North Circular Road, Dublin, Republic of Ireland.

    Tel: (00 353) 1 836 3450
    Website: www.dublinsimon.ie

Scotland

148. Churches Action for the Homeless Keyfund, 10-16 York Place, Perth, PH2 8EP.

    Tel: (01738) 580 188

149. Clackmannanshire CAB Rough Sleepers Rent Deposit Scheme, 47 Drysdale Street, Alloa, Clackmannanshire, FK10 1JA.

    Tel: (01259) 723 880

150. Dumbarton CAB, 6-14 Bridge Street, Dumbarton, G82 1NT.

    Tel: (01389) 765 345

151. East Dunbartonshire Council, Housing Service, Tom Johnston House, Civic Way, Kirkintilloch, G66 4TJ.

    Tel: (0141) 578 8000

152. Falkirk Homeless Project, c/o CAB, Old Sheriff Court, Hope Street, Falkirk, FK1 5AT.

    Tel: (01324) 692 070

153. Fife Keyfund, Open Door Fife, James Street, Dunfermline, Fife, KY12 7QE.

    Tel: (01383) 312960
    Website: www.geocities.com/open doorfife
    Email: opendoorfife@ukonline.co.uk

154. Glasgow Rent Deposit Scheme, Unit 2 Victoria Court, Hollybrook Street, Glasgow, Lanarkshire, G42 7HB.

    Tel: (0141) 423 0232

155. Jubilee Key Scheme, Suite 6, Beech House, 10-18 Hope Street, Hamilton, South Lanarkshire, ML3 6AF.

Tel: (01698) 891 551

156. Matthews Smartmove Project, Edinburgh Cyrenians, Norton Park, 57 Albion Road, Edinburgh, EH7 5QY.

Tel: (0131) 475 2356

157. McKay SmartMove Project, Dundee Cyrenians, 10 Brewery Lane, Dundee, DD1 5QW.

Tel: (01382) 228 733

158. Scottish Churches Housing Agency, 28 Albany Street, Edinburgh, EH1 3QH.

Tel: (0131) 477 4500
Email: scotchho@ednet.co.uk

159. SeAscape, 13 Old Bridge Street, Ayr, KA7 1QA.

Tel: (01292) 285 424
Website: www.south-ayrshire.gov.uk

160. Shetland Rent Deposit Scheme, Shetland Islands Council, Housing Services, Fort Road, Lerwick, Shetland, ZE1 0LR.

Tel: (01595) 744 360

161. SmartMove (East Lothian), Tolbooth Gate, 57 Market Street, Haddington, East Lothian, EH41 3JG.

Tel: (01620) 829 300

162. Stirling Rent Deposit Guarantee Scheme, Patrons of Cowane's Hospital, 49 St John Street, Stirling, FK8 1ED.

Tel: (01786) 472 247
Email: rdgs@cowanes.org.uk

Wales

163. Agorfa Bond Scheme, Greenhouse, 1 Trevelyan Terrace, High Street, Bangor, Gwynedd, LL57 1AX.

Tel: (01248) 355 058
Website: www.kbe51.dial.pipex.com

164. Barnardos Cymru, Compass for Young People, Wrexham Victoria Youth Centre, 13 Hill Street, Wrexham, LL11 1SN.

Tel: (01978) 315 130
Email: compass@barnardos.org.uk

165. Cardiff Bond Board, 109 St Mary Street, Cardiff, CF10 1DX.

Tel: (029) 2087 1442
Website: www.cardiff-bond-board. org.uk
Email: cbb@cardiff-bond-boar.org.uk

166. Bridgend Bond Board, Barbados Open Door Project, 2nd Floor, Assembly Building, 16-18 Derwen Road, Bridgend, CF31 1LH.

Tel: (01656) 668 834

167. Carmarthenshire Bond Scheme, 5 Spilman Street, Carmarthen, SA31 1LE.

Tel: (01267) 228 937

168. Ceredigion Care Society, Agoriad Housing Bond Scheme, 26 Cambrian Street, Aberystwyth Dyfed, SY23 1NZ.

Tel: (01970) 639 111

169. Denbighshire Bond Board, c/o Community Agency, Station House, Bodfor Street, Rhyl, Denbighshire, LL18 1AT.

   Tel: (01745) 343 342
   Email: rhyl.community@ denbighshire.gov.uk

170. Dewis Housing Association, 47 Station Road, Port Talbot, West Glamorgan, SA13 1NW.

   Tel: (01639) 882 536

171. Ebbw Fach Development Trust, Nantyglo Institute, New Road, Nantyglo, Blaenau Gwent, NP23 4JT.

   Tel: (01495) 315 055

172. Llamau Housing Society, Suite B1, Canton House, 435-451 Cowbridge Road East, Cardiff, CF5 1JH.

   Tel: (029) 2023 9585

173. Merthyr Bond Board, 56 High Street, Pontmorlais, Merthyr Tydfil, CF47 8UN.

   Tel: (01685) 382 422

174. NashMove Bond Guarantee Scheme, Rehousing Services Office, The Bus Station, Newport, NP20 1EY.

   Tel: (01633) 232 594
   Website: www.nash01.org.uk/ nm.html

175. Pembrokeshire Action for the Homeless (PATH), 20 Upper Market Street, Haverfordwest, Pembrokeshire, SA61 1QA.

   Tel: (01437) 765 335
   Website: www.pash-homeless.co.uk
   Email: pemcare@btconnect.com

176. Rhondda Cynon Taff Bond Board, Housing Advice Centre, 35a Taff Street, Pontypridd, South Wales, CF37 4YY.

   Tel: (01443) 485 515
   Website: www.rhondda-cynon-taff. gov.uk

177. Right Move, Monmouthshire County Council, Housing Dept., County Hall, Cwmbran, NP44 2XH.

   Tel: (01633) 644 472
   Website: www.monmouthshire.gov.uk
   Email: socialandhousingservies@ monmouthshire.gov.uk

178. Swansea SmartMove, Barnados Wales, Swansea Bond, Board Bays Project, 32-36 High Street, Swansea, SA1 1LF.

   Tel: (01792) 455 105

vi) List of hotspots

What is a hotspot?

First of all we need to define a hotspot. A hotspot is an area where there are properties available for sale that fall into one of these three categories:

Gold – Property prices are predicted to rise at a greater rate than the national average <u>and</u> the rental yield is greater than the national average.

Silver – The rental yield is greater than the national average.

Bronze – Property prices are predicted to rise at a greater rate than the national average.

I have ranked the categories with Gold being the most desirable as Gold enjoys the best of both worlds – capital growth and yield thus spreading the return and overall risk. Silver is ranked second as the yield is a certain outcome whereas the capital growth for Bronze is uncertain.

I've found in my experience that investors do choose categories Gold, Silver or Bronze on personal circumstances but rely more so on gut reaction. My advice is to choose all of them! There is no need to place all your eggs in one basket. Property is a relatively safe investment but there is a degree of uncertainty so if possible, by investing in all the categories above, you eliminate some of the business risk.

Identification of a hotspot

So how did I identify the hotspots listed? Well the categories are based on two factors:

1. Actual rental yields
2. Predicted property prices

1. Actual rental yields

The first factor, actual rental yields, was easy to do. Actual rental yield is:

$$\frac{\text{actual yearly rent}}{\text{actual property price}}$$

Since these figures are actuals, I collated all the rental figures from local letting agents in the UK; all the local property prices in the UK from the Land Registry; and calculated all the yields being offered from all UK locations. I then eliminated all the poor yielding locations where I thought tenant demand was low (even if they were high yielding).

2. Predicted property prices

Here I did not predict the property prices as this is an impossible thing to do. If I could, I would not be writing this book but buying everything I could in a hotspot area! All I did was look at what would make an area's property price rise above the national average. I came up with the following:

- Proposed transportation link improvements such as improved road and rail links, expansion of local airports and improved public transport.
- Proposed inward investment from private companies, government and trusts.
- Proposed improvements to leisure facilities such as sport centres, parks and shopping centres.
- The likelihood of holiday seasons being lengthened for holiday areas.
- My own experience gathered from being in this industry and from comments from letting and estate agents.

My top 10

All these areas are category Gold and are listed in alphabetical order.

Area: **Bethnal Green, London, E2**

Crime (per 1,000 population):
Violence – 34; Sexual – 2; Burglary – 10; Motor – 12

Yield range: 6.2-9.9%

Price ranges:
Studio flat: Low £ – 87,000; High £ – 97,000; Low £pw – 135; High £pw – 185; Low – 8.1%; High – 9.9%

1 bed flat: Low £ – 95,000; High £ – 175,000; Low £pw – 175; High £pw – 260; Low – 7.7%; High – 9.5%

2 bed flat: Low £ – 145,000; High £ – 280,000; Low £pw – 210; High £pw – 360; Low – 6.7%; High – 7.5%

2 bed house: Low £ – 210,000; High £ – 310,000; Low £pw – 260; High £pw – 420; Low – 6.4%; High – 7.0%

3 bed house: Low £ – 260,000; High £ – 400,000; Low £pw – 310; High £pw – 490; Low – 6.2%; High – 6.4%

Valuations above the London average by: -9.2% (£206,425)

Capital growth last 12 months: Actual – 44%; National average – 18%

Capital growth last 4 years: Actual – 102%; National average – 74%

Demand for letting: Excellent

Average void period: 7 days

Score: Total (out of 10) – **8**; Capital growth (out of 5) – 4; Yield (out of 5) – 4

Summary: Extremely close to the City with excellent rental yields – could be the next 'Farringdon'.

Description: I find this place amazing. It is a £3 cab ride or a three-minute tube journey and you are in the heart of the financial capital of the world! Yet the area looks run down in places with only a few pockets of 'nice' areas. The nice areas being the old ex-local authority Victorian flats such as Corfield Street, off Bethnal Green Road, which are no more than five storeys high, loft conversion flats springing up by developers from disused schools and warehouses and newly builds such as Millennium Place, opposite Cambridge Heath Station.

These areas are highly sought after by the young professionals who work in the city. This has led to both property and rental prices rising in proportion with each other, hence the decent yields of nearly 10% in some areas. I think that these young professionals do not mind taking the risk in living in these east-end ex-gangster type of areas as they get a lot more for their money. Shoreditch is only a brief stroll down Bethnal Green Road and there they enter into the trendy-bar city where other young professional 20-somethings meet up.

Tenant demand will be strong if our financial economy is flourishing as this area relies on jobs being provided by the City. Currently the state of the financial economy seems OK for at least the next 12 months but be aware that this can change quite rapidly. In the last six years the number of jobs in London have grown by 17% but we are heavily linked to the US economy so it pays to keep abreast of what's going on across the Atlantic.

Queen Mary's Hospital & College is a five-minute walk and hence the area proves to be popular with medical students. The college is keen to hear from landlords as there is a shortage of student accommodation and it offers a fee-free tenant finding service.

I think out of all the areas in London this area will be radically different in 20 years to what it is today. It is ripe for gentrification and is close enough to the burgeoning financial city to be gobbled up and turned into a support centre of hotels, restaurants and bars for international business visitors.

Tube: Bethnal Green. Central Line – Zone 2. Three minutes to Liverpool Street.

Area: **Corby, Northamptonshire, NN18**

Population aged 15+: 39,311

Percentage class ABC1: Actual – 33%; National average – 44%

Crime (per 1,000 population): Violence – 17; Sexual – 1; Burglary – 8; Motor – 11

Yield range: 4.5-12.9%

Price ranges:
Flats & maisonettes: Low £ – 26,184; High £ – 40,112; Low £pw – 65; High £pw – 85; Low – 11%; High – 12.9%

Terraced: Low £ – 46,371; High £ – 60,836; Low £pw – 70; High £pw – 88; Low – 7.5%; High – 7.8%

Semi-detached: Low £ – 49,873; High £ – 58,414; Low £pw – 78; High £pw – 92; Low – 8.1%; High – 8.2%

Detached: Low £ – 115,831; High £ – 120,175; Low £pw – 100; High £pw – 140; Low – 6.0%; High – 4.5%

Capital growth last 12 months: Actual – 20%; National average – 18%

Capital growth last 4 years: Actual – 80%; National average – 74%

Large employers in the area: RS Components, Oxford University Press and Avon Cosmetics

Demand for letting: Excellent

Average void period: 5 days

Score: Total (out of 10) – **10**; Capital growth (out of 5) – 5; Yield (out of 5) – 5

Summary: Landing ground in England for the Scottish which keeps tenant demand high.

Description: Corby was home to the big steel and iron industries which employed a significant proportion of the population but they closed down in the 1980s. This resulted in high unemployment initially but it has partly recovered with the arrival of a number of smaller manufacturing and distribution industries.

I have 20 properties in this area. Due to the above average unemployment a lot of my properties are let to DSS claimants. Corby is a new town so there are plenty of ex-local authority flats and homes for sale in order to meet this demand.

My experience with the council is a mixed one – sometimes they process the benefit applications efficiently and sometimes not. I have had to wait for payments to come through for up to 20 weeks! The council has been getting assistance recently and processing times are improving.

Tenant demand is strong. If I put an advert in the local press I will get at least 10 calls and the property will be let within the week. There is a high Scottish population and many who wish to move to England come to Corby first.

Mainline railway station: None. Corby bus station to Peterborough train station. Peterborough is one hour to London.

Road access: A14. 90 miles to London and 60 miles to Birmingham.

Local newspaper: The Citizen & Evening Telegraph – Tel: (01536) 506 100

Area: **Derby, Derbyshire, DE1**

Population aged 15+: 199,476

Percentage class ABC1: Actual – 46%; National average – 44%

Crime (per 1,000 population):
Violence – 16; Sexual – 1; Burglary – 11; Motor – 5

Yield range: 4.9-10.6%

Price ranges:
Flats & maisonettes: Low £ – 28,639; High

£ – 39,305; Low £pw – 50; High £pw – 80; Low – 9%; High – 10.6%

Terraced: Low £ – 63,705; High £ – 96,938; Low £pw – 60; High £pw – 95; Low – 4.9%; High – 5.1%

Semi-detached: Low £ – 73,342; High £ – 93,550; Low £pw – 90; High £pw – 115; Low – 6.4%; High – 6.4%

Capital growth last 12 months: Actual – 24%; National average – 18%

Capital growth last 4 years: Actual – 73%; National average – 74%

Large employers in the area: Acordis Acetate Chemicals Ltd, AEA Technology plc, Balfour Beatty & Co Ltd, Bemrose Security & Printing, Bombardier Transportation, Bonar Teich plc, Delta Crompton Cables Ltd, Midland Mainline (Headquarters), Pektron Ltd, Prudential Banking plc (Egg), Reckitt Benckiser, Rolls-Royce plc, Royal Crown Derby Porcelain Co Ltd, S&A Foods Ltd, Scholl (UK) Ltd, Shaw Group UK Ltd, SIG Packaging, Software AG, Toyota Motor Manufacturing (UK) Ltd and W S Atkins Rail Ltd

Demand for letting: Good

Average void period: 8 days

Score: Total (out of 10) – 7; Capital growth (out of 5) – 4; Yield (out of 5) – 3

Summary: Toyota's investment in Derbyshire will ensure strong tenant demand for the next 10 years at least.

Description: The decision by Toyota to invest £1.5bn in its European production facility close to Derby has seen further investment in the transport manufacturing sector. Output levels from the Burnaston factory have reached 200,000 cars a year and Toyota now employs over 3,100 people at Burnaston. This has sustained demand for rental properties in Derby and will continue to do so.

The city has a diverse and active economy with a level of performance equal to any other in the East Midlands. Derby has seen its traditional employment base shift towards the service sector over the past decade, an example being the recent call centre investment by Prudential Banking plc (Egg).

Its central location is highly desirable for distribution purposes as it has access to all the key markets in the UK. Population is set to grow by four per cent by 2006 and unemployment is currently falling due to the many number of companies locating to Derby.

Mainline railway station: Derby. One hour 49 minutes to London.

Road access: M1. 130 miles to Greater London.

Local newspaper: Derby Express Series – Tel: (01332) 292 222
Derby Evening Telegraph – Tel: (01332) 291 111

Area: **Grimsby, Lincolnshire, DN31**

Population aged 15+: 68,647

Percentage class ABC1: Actual – 39%; National average – 44%

Crime (per 1,000 population):
Violence – 13; Sexual – 1; Burglary – 17; Motor – 12

Yield range: 8.6-13.6%

Price ranges:
Flats & maisonettes: Low £ – 22,940; High £ – 34,829; Low £pw – 60; High £pw – 90; Low – 13.4%; High – 13.6%

Terraced: Low £ – 25,384; High £ – 41,113; Low £pw – 65; High £pw – 85; Low – 10.8%; High – 13.3%

Semi-detached: Low £ – 36,392; High £ – 54,285; Low £pw – 70; High £pw – 90; Low – 8.6%; High – 10%

Capital growth last 12 months: Actual – 9%; National average – 18%

Capital growth last 4 years: Actual – 33%; National average – 74%

Large employers in the area: NELC, Youngs Bluecrest, Heinz, Baxters, Birds Eye Walls, Novartis, Ciba, Acordis, Frigoscandia, Volkswagen Audi Group, DFDS Tor-Line, BOC and Stora

Demand for letting: Good

Average void period: 10 days

Score: Total (out of 10) – **6**; Capital growth (out of 5) – 1; Yield (out of 5) – 5

Summary: Good yields with good communications.

Description: Once famous for its fishing industry, Grimsby has carved a new identity in recent years as a centre for food processing, pharmaceuticals and petrochemicals. It is also famous for coming top in Dun & Bradstreet's survey, which showed that 88.5% of Grimsby's businesses are profitable – the highest in the country.

Unemployment is high, at 5.2%, compared to the national average of 3.2%, so this area will appeal to the investor who doesn't mind having DSS claimants as tenants.

The area is well connected. It is less than three hours to London by rail and is only a four-minute drive to Humberside Airport. The Humber Bridge can get you to the ferry port in Hull in less than an hour and is a gateway to the area.

Mainline railway station: Grimsby Town. Two hours to York.

Road access: Main access A16 & A46. 36 miles north east of Lincoln. 21 miles from M180.

Local newspaper: Grimsby Evening Telegraph – Tel: (01472) 360 360

Area: **Mansfield, Nottingham, NG18**

Population aged 15+: 65,427

Percentage class ABC1: Actual – 44%; National average – 44%

Crime (per 1,000 population): Violence – 20; Sexual – 1; Burglary – 16; Motor – 8

Yield range: 5.5-13.8%

Price ranges:
Terraced: Low £ – 28,693; High £ – 35,916; Low £pw – 70; High £pw – 95; Low – 12.6%; High – 13.8%

Semi-detached: Low £ – 42,392; High £ – 71,218; Low £pw – 90; High £pw – 120; Low – 11%; High – 8.8%

Detached: Low £ – 67,483; High £ – 146,032; Low £pw – 110; High £pw – 155; Low – 5.5%; High – 8.5%

Capital growth last 12 months: Actual – 3%; National average – 18%

Capital growth last 4 years: Actual – 16%; National average – 74%

Large employers in the area: Plastek, Toray Textiles Europe Ltd, Kyoshin Europe, SPS Aerospace, Label Vision Ltd, Miles Royston Glenair International Ltd, Eften Europa UK Ltd, Multi Arc Uk Ltd, Personna International Ltd and Kappler UK

Demand for letting: Good

Average void period: 14 days

Score: Total (out of 10) – **10**; Capital growth (out of 5) – 5; Yield (out of 5) – 5

Summary: Capital growth very likely with superb yields – what more do you want!

Description: This area has not seen a boom in prices over the last four years and yet still provides excellent value for any property investor. There is a ready supply of terraced houses to purchase with good yields. This area is ripe for capital growth and is next on my list of places for me to personally invest.

Unemployment is above average so demand will exist from DSS benefit applicants. However, planning permission has been granted for the development of a site for businesses at Abbot Road which will provide 1,000 jobs. This will provide a well needed boost for the area and local economy.

Mainline railway station: Mansfield. Two hours 30 minutes to London.

Road access: M1. 141 miles to London and 59 miles to Leeds.

Local newspaper: Mansfield & Ashfield Recorder – Tel: (01623) 420 000
Mansfield & Sutton Observer – Tel: (01623) 465 555
Mansfield CHAD – Tel: (01623) 456 789

Area: **Neath Port Talbot, Glamorgan, South Wales, SA11**

Population aged 15+: 53,815

Percentage class ABC1: Actual – 41%; National average – 44%

Crime (per 1,000 population):
Violence – 10; Sexual – 1; Burglary – 5; Motor – 9

Yield range: 6.9-14%

Price ranges:
Terraced: Low £ – 26,000; High £ – 44,530; Low £pw – 70; High £pw – 90; Low – 10.5%; High – 14%

Semi-detached: Low £ – 37,645; High £ – 62,027; Low £pw – 80; High £pw – 95; Low – 8%; High – 11%

Detached: Low £ – 74,966; High £ – 113,116; Low £pw – 100; High £pw – 150; Low – 6.9%; High – 6.9%

Capital growth last 12 months: Actual – -6%; National average – 18%

Capital growth last 4 years: Actual – 12%; National average – 74%

Large employers in the area: Corus, General Electric, Hi-Lex Cable Systems Ltd, TRW Steering Systems, Visteon Automotive Systems, Orion Electric (UK) Ltd, BP Chemicals, Sumitomo Electric, Envases (UK) Ltd, Carnaud Metalbox Food Can Components, Toyoda TRW Steering Pumps, Borg Warner Automotive, Panasonic, Cornelius Electronics, Excel Electronic Assemblies and Tedeco

Demand for letting: OK

Average void period: 11 days

Score: Total (out of 10) – **10**; Capital growth (out of 5) – 5; Yield (out of 5) – 5

Summary: Excellent opportunity to reap above average returns through capital growth.

Description: Neath has higher than average wages with lower than average property prices, hence the area could afford an increase in property prices.

Neath's economy today is much more diversified with light industry replacing the heavy industrial sector. New inward investment has been secured from both the UK and overseas and growth has been achieved through infrastructure developments and innovative approaches to business support services.

Corus (formally British Steel), employing in excess of 3,000, remains the largest industrial employer in the county borough and a major contributor to the local economy.

The tourism industry contributes significantly to the local economy, attracting over 1.4 million people to its main tourist attractions and bringing an estimated £23 million into the local authority.

The service sector is becoming increasingly important to the local economy, and the opportunity for growth in this sector is good, with a number of good quality sites already established and further developments proposed.

Mainline railway station: Neath. 45 minutes to Cardiff.

Road access: M4. 189 miles to London and 41 miles to Cardiff.

Local newspaper: South Wales Evening Post – Tel: (01792) 650 841
Neath & Port Talbot Guardian – Tel: (029) 2022 3333

Area: **Huddersfield, Yorkshire, HD1**

Population aged 15+: 108,819

Percentage class ABC1: Actual – 41%; National average – 44%

Crime (per 1,000 population):
Violence – 8; Sexual – 1; Burglary – 12; Motor – 8

Yield range: 5.6-14.4%

Price ranges:
Flats & maisonettes: Low £ – 89,650; High £ – 120,028; Low £pw – 140; High £pw – 180; Low – 7.8%; High – 8.1%

Terraced: Low £ – 28,831; High £ – 51,786; Low £pw – 80; High £pw – 100; Low – 10%; High – 14.4%

Semi-detached: Low £ – 92,800; High £ – 103,000; Low £pw – 100; High £pw – 145; Low – 5.6%; High – 7.3%

Capital growth last 12 months: Actual – -1%; National average – 18%

Capital growth last 4 years: Actual – 4%; National average – 74%

Large employers in the area: Boots, Asda and the university

Demand for letting: Good

Average void period: 9 days

Score: Total (out of 10) – **8**; Capital growth (out of 5) – 4; Yield (out of 5) – 4

Summary: Fast growing commuter area that is still cheap.

Description: Over the next ten years, the total population of Kirklees is forecast to grow by 4% – the highest growth rate in West Yorkshire. Huddersfield University is anticipating an increase in the number of students over the decade, which will have a positive impact on the local service sector and on housing demand.

Huddersfield is a commuter area for people working in Leeds. Property prices in Leeds are significantly higher than Huddersfield so the possibility for capital growth is high due to workers in Leeds being priced out.

There is a readily available stock of housing in Huddersfield so if you are looking to build a portfolio quickly, you will have no problem here. Unemployment is higher than the national average so the DSS market is large.

Mainline railway station: Huddersfield. 34 minutes to Manchester and 2 hours 50 minutes to London.

Road access: M62. 29 miles to Manchester and 222 miles to London.

Local newspaper: Huddersfield Weekly News – Tel: (01484) 430 000

Area: **Salford, Manchester, M6**

Population aged 15+: 74,129

Percentage class ABC1: Actual – 39%; National average – 44%

Crime (per 1,000 population):
Violence – 14; Sexual – 1; Burglary – 20; Motor – 15

Yield range: 7.9-26.6%

Price ranges:
Terraced: Low £ – 14,630; High £ – 58,237; Low £pw – 75; High £pw – 110; Low – 9.8%; High – 26.6%

Semi-detached: Low £ – 33,666; High £ – 81,972; Low £pw – 85; High £pw – 125; Low – 13.1%; High – 7.9%

Capital growth last 12 months: Actual – 14%; National average – 18%

Capital growth last 4 years: Actual – 36%; National average – 74%

Large employers in the area: The Inland Revenue and the university

Demand for letting: OK

Average void period: 18 days

Score: Total (out of 10) – **8**; Capital growth (out of 5) – 3; Yield (out of 5) – 5

Summary: Superb yields in a growing city.

Description: Salford's location in the heart of Greater Manchester provides access to a large domestic market of over 2.5million. Salford's economy is an open one. A considerable proportion of Salford's population continues to work outside the city (41%), particularly in the Regional Centre and Trafford Park.

Unemployment in Salford has hit a 17-year low. Latest statistics show that the unemployment rate in the city stands at 3.9%, which is below average for the UK.

The city, together with Salford University and the RDA, is developing its Innovation Park and this is expected to support companies including inward investors and a growing number of spinouts from the university. The city is expected to grow by 6.5% by 2008.

The yields are fantastic, up to 27% in the not so good areas, hence competition is fierce so expect longer void periods.

Mainline railway station: Salford Central. Three hours 21 minutes to London.

Road access: M602. 215 miles to London and 93 miles to Birmingham.

Local newspaper: Salford Advertiser – Tel: (0161) 789 5015

Area: **Stockton-on-Tees, Cleveland, TS18**

Population aged 15+: 139,959

Percentage class ABC1: Actual – 31%; National average – 44%

Crime (per 1,000 population):
Violence – 4; Sexual – 1; Burglary – 2;
Motor – 6

Yield range: 5-9.7%

Price ranges:
Terraced: Low £ – 34,831; High £ –
52,994; Low £pw – 65; High £pw – 85;
Low – 8.3%; High – 9.7%

Semi-detached: Low £ – 60,175; High £ –
76,780; Low £pw – 80; High £pw – 110;
Low – 6.9%; High – 7.4%

Detached: Low £ – 97,028; High £ –
149,912; Low £pw – 100; High £pw – 145;
Low – 5.0%; High – 5.3%

Capital growth last 12 months: Actual –
-15%; National average – 18%

Capital growth last 4 years: Actual – 31%;
National average – 74%

Large employers in the area: Sanyo,
Samsung, BASF and Armstrong World
Industries

Demand for letting: Good

Average void period: 10 days

Score: Total (out of 10) – 7;
Capital growth (out of 5) – 5; Yield (out of
5) – 2

Summary: Potentially a very high capital
growth area.

Description: I think that there will be above
average property price growth in this area
which will compensate for the sub 12%
yields. There has been major inward
investment for the creation of several
commercial sites including Teesdale, Belasis

Hall Technology Park and Chemplex. This
can only mean strong demand for rental
properties for people on short- to medium-
term contracts.

The riverside town centre is thriving with
more than 30 medium-to-large enterprises
locating from overseas who are establishing
new manufacturing, retail, office and
storage facilities. This includes Samsung's
£500 million investment alone.

There is plenty of demand from the
university sector, if you wish to enter this
market, from the University of Teeside and
the Stockton campus for the University of
Durham. It is worth contacting the
universities as they offer a free service to
landlords placing students in private rented
properties.

Mainline railway station: Stockton. Three
hours 42 minutes to London.

Road access: A19 & A66. 275 miles to
London. 66 miles to Leeds.

Local newspaper: East Cleveland Herald &
Post – Tel: (01642) 245 401

Area: **Stoke-on-Trent, Staffordshire, ST6**

Population aged 15+: 19,298

Percentage class ABC1: Actual – 37%;
National average – 44%

Crime (per 1,000 population):
Violence – 25; Sexual – 1; Burglary – 12;
Motor – 9

Yield range: 4.7-16.4%

Price ranges:
Terraced: Low £ – 18,993; High £ –

38,118; Low £pw – 60; High £pw – 90; Low – 12.3%; High – 16.4%

Semi-detached: Low £ – 38,166; High £ – 56,306; Low £pw – 75; High £pw – 105; Low – 10.2%; High – 9.7%

Detached: Low £ – 89,161; High £ – 123,959; Low £pw – 80; High £pw – 150; Low – 6.3%; High – 4.7%

Capital growth last 12 months: Actual – 5%; National average – 18%

Capital growth last 5 years: Actual – 29%; National average – 80%

Large employers in the area: Caudwell Communications, Michelin, Waterford Wedgwood, Spode, Royal Doulton and H & R Johnson Tiles

Demand for letting: Good

Average void period: 12 days

Score: Total (out of 10) – **8**; Capital growth (out of 5) – 3; Yield (out of 5) – 5

Summary: Relatively untapped market by investors which has kept property prices low.

Description: This city has six major towns in the area – Burslem, Fenton, Hanley, Longton, Stoke and Tunstall. All these areas offer cheap and affordable investment properties with decent yields. I intend to buy 40 properties in this area this year alone.

The city is in the heart of the ceramics industry and includes the headquarters and manufacturing bases of most of the UK's leading pottery companies. It is also home to centres of excellence such as the British Ceramic Confederation, CERAM Research and the Hothouse Centre for Design. This concentration of manufacturers and support organisations provides the basis for the local economy. Four million people visit the city every year because of the potteries and this provides over 5,000 jobs for the local economy.

Plenty of new jobs have been created recently in the service sector – mainly call centres and logistics reflecting the city's large catchment area workforce and road links. Unemployment is slightly above average at 4% (UK average 3.4%) but I do not think this has a significant effect on the local economy.

Stoke-on-Trent is a city undergoing change. Its availability to cheap and skilled labour, its location and growing university are helping to create a new thriving city.

It is in the centre of the country, midway between Manchester and Birmingham and has excellent communications. New transport links have opened up prime development sites for inward commercial investors. Significant new investment has seen the city centre firmly established as the shopping and cultural centre for the region. Leading high street names are found in and around the award winning Potteries Centre, and major show and events are hosted in the city's theatres.

Mainline railway station: Stoke-on-Trent. One hour 50 minutes to London, one hour to Birmingham and 50 minutes to Manchester.

Local newspaper: The Sentinel –
Tel: (01782) 602 525

The rest of the hotspots listed below are Silver and Bronze. As a rule of thumb, London and the Home Counties are Bronze and the rest are Silver.

England East Anglia

1. Attleborough, Norfolk
2. Boston, Lincolnshire
3. Brookenby, Lincolnshire
4. Bungay, Norfolk
5. Chatteris, Cambridgeshire
6. Cromer, Norfolk
7. Downham Market, Norfolk
8. Eye, Suffolk
9. Grantham, Lincolnshire
10. Hadleigh, Suffolk
11. Ipswich, Suffolk
12. Kings Lynn, Norfolk
13. Lincoln, Lincolnshire
14. Market Rasen, Lincolnshire
15. Mundesley, Norfolk
16. Norwich, Norfolk
17. Orton Goldhay, Peterborough
18. Orton Malbourne, Peterborough
19. St Neots, Cambridgeshire
20. Skegness, Lincolnshire
21. Sudbury, Suffolk
22. Welland, Peterborough
23. Wickham Market, Woodbridge, Suffolk
24. Wisbech, Cambridgeshire

England Essex, Herts and Middlesex

1. Aveley, Essex
2. Basildon, Essex
3. Clacton-on-Sea, Essex
4. Colchester, Essex
5. Dagenham, Essex
6. East Tilbury, Essex
7. Enfield, Middlesex
8. Frinton-on-Sea, Essex
9. Grays, Essex
10. Halstead, Essex
11. Harlow, Essex
12. Harold Hill, Essex
13. Harwich, Essex
14. Hornchurch, Essex
15. Laindon, Essex
16. Pitsea, Essex
17. Purfleet, Essex
18. Rainham, Essex
19. Romford, Essex
20. Sawbridgeworth, Herts
21. Sheerness, Essex

22. Shoeburyness, Essex
23. South Ockendon, Essex
24. Southend, Essex
25. Stanford Le Hope, Essex
26. Tilbury, Essex
27. Waltham Cross, Herts
28. Westcliffe-on-Sea, Essex
29. Wickford, Essex
30. Witham, Essex

England London

1. Beckton
2. Bexley Heath
3. Leyton
4. Northolt
5. Plaistow
6. Streatham
7. Thamesmead
8. Walthamstow
9. West Hendon
10. Woolwich

England Mid North

1. Balby, Doncaster
2. Beeston, Leeds
3. Castleford
4. Crossgates, Leeds
5. Dewsbury

6. Garforth
7. Goole
8. Hull
9. Marsden, Yorkshire
10. Pocklington, Yorkshire
11. Rochdale, Lancashire
12. Rotherham
13. Roundhay
14. Scarborough, Yorkshire
15. Scunthorpe
16. Skipton, Bradford
17. Wakefield, Yorks

England Midlands

1. Anstey Heights, Leicester
2. Aspley, Notts
3. Bedford, Bedfordshire
4. Bestwood, Notts
5. Bilborough, Notts
6. Binley, Coventry
7. Bobbersmill, Notts
8. Braunstone, Leicester
9. Broxtowe, Notts
10. Bulwell, Notts
11. Burton-on-Trent, Staffordshire
12. Camphill, Northants
13. Clifton, Notts

14. Daventry, Warwickshire
15. Dunstable, Bedfordshire
16. Foleshill, Coventry
17. Highbury Vale, Notts
18. Hodge Hill, Birmingham
19. Ilkeston, Notts
20. Irthlingborough, Northants
21. Kettering, Northants
22. Kimberley, Notts
23. Kirkby-in-Ashfield, Notts
24. Leicester City Centre, Leicestershire
25. Luton, Bedfordshire
26. Moulton, Northants
27. Newark, Notts
28. Newcastle-under-Lyme, Staffordshire
29. Newstead Village, Hucknall, Notts
30. Northampton, Northants
31. Oldbury, West Midlands
32. Rednal, Birmingham
33. Rugby, Warwickshire
34. Rushden, Northants
35. Shrewsbury
36. Strelley, Notts
37. Sutton-in-Ashfield, Notts
38. The Meadows, Notts
39. Thorneywood, Notts

40. Thorpelands, Northants
41. Top Valley, Notts
42. Walsall, West Midlands
43. Warren Hill, Notts
44. Wellingborough, Northants
45. Willenhall, Coventry
46. Wolverhampton, West Midlands

England North East

1. Arthurs Hill, Newcastle
2. Benwell, Newcastle
3. Bishop Auckland, Darlington
4. Blakelaw, West Denton
5. Blyth, Newcastle
6. Carlisle, Northumberland
7. Chilton, Darlington
8. Colliery, Durham
9. Consett
10. Elswick, Tyne & Wear
11. Ferryhill, Spennymoor
12. Gateshead, Newcastle
13. Hartlepool
14. Hebburn
15. Hendon, Sunderland
16. Hexham, Northumberland
17. Houghton-le-Spring
18. Lemington, West Denton

19. Middlesborough, Cleveland
20. Newcastle-upon-Tyne, Northumberland
21. Newton Aycliffe, Darlington
22. Prudhoe, Northumberland
23. Redcar, Cleveland
24. Ryton, Crawcrook
25. Seaham
26. South Shields, Newcastle
27. Walkergate, Tyne & Wear
28. Wallsend, Newcastle
29. Washington, Tyne & Wear

England North West

1. Accrington
2. Allerton, Liverpool
3. Bacup, Manchester
4. Barnsley, Lancashire
5. Birkenhead, Lancashire
6. Blackburn
7. Blackpool
8. Bolton
9. Bootle, Liverpool
10. Bradford
11. Broughton, Cheshire
12. Bury, Lancashire
13. Chester, Cheshire
14. Clayton, Manchester
15. Colne, Lancashire
16. Crewe, Cheshire
17. Darwen, Lancashire
18. Denton, Manchester
19. Dudley
20. Eccles, Manchester
21. Eddington, Doncaster
22. Farnworth, Lancashire
23. Gainsborough, Manchester
24. Golborne, Cheshire
25. Halifax
26. Holywell, Flintshire,
27. Huyton, Prescot
28. Hyde Park, Manchester
29. Keighley
30. Kirkby, Maghull
31. Leigh, Lancashire
32. Liverpool, L4
33. Liverpool, L6
34. Liverpool, L7
35. Liverpool, L8
36. Liverpool, L9
37. Liverpool, L13
38. Liverpool, L14
39. Liverpool, L20

40. Longsight, Manchester
41. Mexborough
42. Morecambe, Lancashire
43. Moss Side, Manchester
44. Northwich, Cheshire
45. Openshaw, Manchester
46. Peasley Cross, Merseyside
47. Preston
48. Rishton, Lancashire
49. Rock Ferry, Bebington
50. Rotherham
51. Runcorn, Cheshire
52. Rusholme, Manchester
53. St Helens, Merseyside
54. Sheffield City Centre
55. Swinton, Manchester
56. Wallasey
57. Walton Vale, Lancashire
58. Warrington, Lancashire
59. Waterloo, Lancashire
60. West Derby
61. Wigan
62. Winsford, Cheshire
63. Withlington, Manchester
64. Wombwell
65. Worksop, Manchester
66. Worsley, Manchester

England South

1. Bexhill-on-sea, Sussex
2. Bognor Regis, Portsmouth
3. Bournemouth, Dorset
4. Fareham, Hampshire
5. Rottingdean, Brighton
6. Rowner, Gosport
7. Ryde, Isle of Wight
8. St Leonards-on-Sea, East Sussex
9. St Marys, Southampton
10. Sandown, Isle of Wight
11. Shirley, Southampton
12. Sholing, Southampton
13. Southbourne, Dorset
14. Southsea, Hampshire
15. Thornhill, Southampton

England South East

1. Ashford, Kent
2. Broadstairs, Kent
3. Canterbury, Kent
4. Chatham, Kent
5. Cliftonville, Kent
6. Dartford, Kent
7. Dover, Kent
8. Eastbourne, Sussex

9. Erith, Kent
10. Faversham, Kent
11. Folkstone, Kent
12. Hastings, East Sussex
13. Herne Bay, Kent
14. Margate, Kent
15. Ramsgate, Kent
16. Rochester, Kent
17. Sittingbourne, Kent
18. Snodland, Kent
19. Westgate-on-sea, Kent

England South West

1. Avon, Bristol
2. Axminster, Devon
3. Bodmin, Plymouth
4. Bovey Tracey, Devon
5. Bridgewater, Taunton
6. Callington, Cornwall
7. Chard, Somerset
8. Chelston, Torquay, Devon
9. Clevedon, Bristol
10. Dawlish, Devon
11. Devonport, Plymouth
12. Filton, Bristol
13. Gillingham, Dorset
14. Honicknowle, Plymouth

15. Hooe, Plymouth
16. Houndstone, Somerset
17. Ilfracombe, Devon
18. Ilminster, Somerset
19. Keyham, Plymouth
20. Laira, Plymouth
21. Launceston, Cornwall
22. Lipson, Plymouth
23. Looe, Plymouth
24. Paignton, Devon
25. Plymouth City Centre, Plymouth
26. St Beaudeaux, Plymouth
27. Shepton Mallet, Somerset
28. Stoke, Plymouth
29. Stratton Creber, Newquay
30. Tavistock, Devon
31. Teignmouth, Devon
32. Topsham, Devon
33. Torquay
34. Wellington, Somerset
35. Westbury, Bath
36. Weston Super Mare, Somerset
37. Yeovil, Somerset

England West

1. Caldicot, Gloucs
2. Churchdown, Gloucs

3.   Cinderford, Gloucs

4.   Coleford, Gloucs

5.   Hardwicke, Gloucs

6.   Hereford, Herefordshire

7.   Kidderminster, Worcestershire

8.   Newtown Farm, Herefordshire

9.   Redditch, Worcestershire

10. Tewkesbury, Gloucs

11. Worcester, Worcestershire

Scotland

1.   Airdrie, Lanarkshire

2.   Alexandria, Dumbarton

3.   Beith, Bridge of Weir

4.   Bellshill

5.   Bridgeton, Glasgow

6.   Broxburn, Livingston

7.   Carstairs Junction, Lanarkshire

8.   Chapelhall, Airdrie

9.   Cleland, Lanarkshire

10. Craigshill, Livingston

11. Cronberry, Ayr

12. Dalry, Bridge of Weir

13. Darvel, Kilmarnock

14. Dennistown, Glasgow

15. Dumbarton, Dumbartonshire

16. East Kilbride, Glasgow

17. Falkirk

18. Glengarnock, Bridge of Weir

19. Glenrothes

20. Greenock, Refrewshire

21. Govanhill, Glasgow

22. Hamilton

23. Ibrox, Glasgow

24. Inverheithing, Dalgety Bay

25. Kilbirnie, Bridge of Weir

26. Kilsyth, Glasgow

27. Kilwinning, Troon

28. Kirkcaldy

29. Kirkintolloch, Bishopsbriggs

30. Lochgelly, Dumfermline

31. Maybole, Ayr

32. New Cumnock, Ayr

33. Newmilus, Kilmarnock, Ayrshire

34. North Carbrain, Cumberland

35. Paisley

36. Port Glasgow, Refrewshire

37. Preisthill, Glasgow

38. Saracen Cross, Glasgow

39. Springboig, Glasgow

40. Stewarton, Kilmarnock

41. Tollcross, Glasgow

42. Whitburn, Livingston

43. Wishaw, Lanarkshire

44. Yoker, Glasgow

Wales

1. Abercynon, Pontypridd

2. Abertillery, Ebbw Vale

3. Caerphilly

4. Church Village, Pontypridd

5. Edwardsville, Pontypridd

6. Ely, Rhiwbina

7. Gilfach Goch, Pontypridd

8. Greenfield Terrace, Ebbw Vale

9. Treharris, Pontypridd

vii) List of freefone/lo-call providers

Freephone providers can route your 0800 number to your landline at a cost to you of as little as 3p a minute. You can also route your 0800 number to your mobile for more. Lo-call 0845 numbers are available from the following providers, which means that the caller only pays the cost of a local call. The cost to you is nothing! The reason for this is because the provider wants your volume of calls. There are even some numbers that you get paid per minute (0871 numbers), but only cost the caller a standard national call. Check out some of these providers:

Name: *Crosby Communications*
Tel: (0800) 038 6000
Website: www.crosbycomms.co.uk

Name: *Dataweb Technologies*
Tel: (0845) 130 3944
Website: www.telnos.co.uk

Name: *Dolphin*
Tel: (0800) 195 1255
Website: www.freephoneservices.co.uk

Name: *Efax*
Tel: (0845) 458 2845
Website: www.efax.co.uk

Name: *Future Numbers*
Tel: (0800) 038 8873
Website: www.future-numbers.co.uk

Name: *Global Telecom*
Tel: (0870) 055 5657
Website: www.globaltelecomuk.com

Name: *Phone number shop*
Tel: (0800) 019 2130
Website: www.thephonenumbershop.co.uk

Name: *Planet*
Tel: (0845) 066 6666
Website: www.planet-numbers.co.uk

Name: *Telecom Plus*
Tel: (0800) 074 0782
Website: www.0800-freephone-numbers.co.uk

Name: 21st Century
Tel: (0870) 777 2121
Website: www.21st-centurytelecom.com

viii) List of credit-checking agencies

Here is a list of credit-checking agencies. Some offer guarantees on the rent if the tenant defaults.

Name: *Homelet*
Tel: (0845) 117 6000
Website: www.homeletuk.com
Cost: £17.50 – basic

£39.95 – including employer's reference and landlord's reference.

£99.00 – available if prospective tenant is a full-time employee. If tenant defaults, they guarantee the rent for six months up to £2,000 pcm rent.

From £109.00 - if prospective tenant is part time or self-employed. If tenant defaults, they guarantee the rent for six months.

Name: *Letsure*
Tel: (0870) 077 0800
Website: www.letsure.co.uk
Cost: Varies

Name: *Moneypenny*
Tel: (020) 7730 0883
Website: www.moneypenny.co.uk
Cost: £17.50

Name: *Paragon*
Tel: (0800) 092 5901
Website: www.paragon-plus.co.uk
Cost: £15.00 – basic

£29.00 – including employer's reference and landlord's reference.

£49.00 – available if prospective tenant is a full-time employee. If the tenant defaults, they guarantee the rent for six months up to £1,500 pcm rent.

As you can see from the above, the checks can be expensive. If you put forward four prospective tenants under a guarantee scheme check, you could be spending nearly £300 – and this still doesn't mean that you would have found a tenant as all the tenants could have failed the credit check!

ix) Guaranteed rent and maintenance contracts

Guaranteed rent can be obtained by one of three ways:

1. Via an insurance contract. This is where you pay a percentage of the rent to the insurer, typically three per cent, or a fixed fee to the insurer, to cover you against the tenant defaulting. The tenant has to be credit-checked initially for a nominal fee, but from then on the rent is guaranteed. All the companies listed in the credit-checking agencies, above, provide this service.

2. Obtaining a credit check for a one-off fee and then the rent is guaranteed if the tenant defaults. All the companies listed

in the credit-checking agencies, above, will do this for you.

3. Getting a letting agent or institution to pay the rent direct. Agents called Northwood Lettings www.northwood lettings.co.uk and Your Move www.your-move.co.uk provide this. These are growing chains of national estate agents who pay the rent directly to your bank account, even if the property is vacant. University institutions sometimes pay guaranteed rent, as they can then sublet your property to the students. It is worth contacting the university in the area that you are thinking of buying. Councils are also paying guaranteed rent for asylum seekers or under the 'Empty House Scheme'. This is where the councils will even refurbish the property at no expense to yourself through a government grant (maximum £12,000) in order to make your property tenantable. Schemes that I have found are www.carrick.gov.uk, (01872) 224 400, www.wealden.gov.uk, (01323) 443 378, and www.hastings.gov.uk, (0800) 085 8967. I am sure there are many others.

I have only found one maintenance insurer and that is Homelet (see contact details on page 126). They cover the cost of a contractor's call-out, labour charge, parts and materials up to the cost of £500 including VAT. They use their own contractors, so if there is an emergency you simply call Homelet. They ensure that a contractor will arrive within four hours. The cost for this insurance is £7 per month. This policy does not cover you for call-outs due to lack of routine maintenance.

If you want to obtain your own credit file, then you have to write to both Experian and Equifax. Ensure that you give them your full forename and surname, your date of birth and all addresses you have resided during the past six years. They charge a nominal £2 fee. Their addresses are:

Experian Consumer Help Service
PO Box 8000
Nottingham NG1 5GX

Equifax Credit File Advice Centre
PO Box 1140
Bradford BD1 5US

x) Letting agents

I would suggest that you only use an Association of Residential Letting Agents (ARLA)-accredited member to collect your rent. Since the agent will be handling your money, you need to be covered against fraud i.e. the agent running off with your money! If the agent commits any fraudulent acts your money is fully guaranteed by ARLA. You do not even have to prove the fraud to get your money from ARLA.

Your local ARLA member can be found from www.arla.co.uk or by calling (0845) 345 5752.

The Buy-to-Let Bible

xi) Management software providers

I only really recommend one software provider, EZPZ Landlord. This is because there are few providers of this type of software and this one is the only one that is any good. The great thing about this program is that it is FREE! A fully working program for management of five properties is downloadable from their website free of charge. If you wish to manage more than five, then it will cost you £299. The product details are as follows:

EZPZ Landlord - product details

EZPZ Landlord is a computer book-keeping system designed specifically to help landlords manage their properties. EZPZ Landlord has all the standard accounting features you would expect from a computerised book-keeping system:

- Sales ledger
- Purchase ledger
- Nominal ledger
- Bank reconciliation
- VAT analysis
- Automated entries
- Prepayments and accruals

with additional features including the calculation of rents and automated credit control for tenants. The system enables you to keep details of individual properties and tenants, and the links between them.

Properties

The property records form the main records of the system. Each property will have rent and tenancy records created for it. For example, a tenancy record will hold details of the type of tenancy, its duration and the tenant. Each rent and tenancy record covers a period of time, so the system maintains a history of previous rent rates that have been in force, and the tenants that have occupied the property.

Rents may be based on any charging period such as weekly, calendar-monthly, quarterly, or you can define any non-standard period, and may be charged in advance or arrears.

Tenancies may be created for a property for any period and users may define their own tenancy types if unusual periods are involved. The Expiring Tenancies report shows properties for which the tenancy is due to expire.

Accommodation details may be recorded for each property and you can even store a picture within the property record. An inventory and schedule of condition may be created for each property. These may be used in periodic inspections of a property to assess possible damage by tenants.

Tenants

Each tenant's ledger shows what the tenant owes at any time. The automated credit control feature suggests what action to take based on how long rent charges have been overdue. Statements, reminders and final reminders can all be customised to your own requirements.

Tenancy agreements

Tenancy agreements may be printed for any tenancy with a few clicks of the mouse button. Agreements are created from a database of standard paragraphs that can be

128

added, removed or customised, as you desire.

Reports

The system has a wealth of reports to offer, as you would expect from any book-keeping system. You can prepare a monthly profit and loss account, balance sheet and even carry out VAT analysis if you are VAT registered.

Limitations of use

The demonstration version of the software limits the creation of properties to three. The registered version does not have this limitation. The number of records that may be created, using the registered version, is limited only by the amount of storage space you have.

System requirements

EZPZ Landlord was written using Microsoft Visual FoxPro V6.0 and is designed to run on any stand-alone PC and on any version of Windows including Windows 2000 Professional. To run EZPZ Landlord you will need a minimum of:

- An IBM-compatible computer with a 486 66MHz processor (or higher)
- A mouse
- 16 MB RAM
- 10 MB free space on your hard drive

Support

Free help and support is available by telephone (office hours) and email, for the lifetime of the product.

Ordering

The demonstration version is downloadable free of charge from the website www.ezpzsoftware.co.uk. The demonstration version is also available on CD at a price of £5 to cover production and postage and packaging costs. This cost will be deducted from the cost of the registered version should you wish to upgrade. Payment may be made online by credit or debit card, or by telephone on (01709) 871 056.

xii) Local newspapers

If you do not know the local newspaper in the area where you have just invested, there is a very good site that tells you: www.newspapersoc.org.uk. The Newspapers Society, (020) 7636 7014, will have details such as circulation figures, demographics and telephone numbers for you to place your advert.

xiii) List of auctioneers

1. *Allsop & Co*
    100 Knightsbridge,
    London, SW1X 7LB.

    Tel: (020) 7584 6106

2. *Andrews & Robertson*
    27 Camberwell Green,
    London, SE5 7AN.

    Tel: (020) 7703 2662

3. *Athawes Son & Co.*
    The Auctioneers Offices,
    203 High Street, London, W3 9DR.

    Tel: (020) 8992 0056

4.   *Barnard Marcus*
      64-66 Glenthorne Road, London,
      W6 0LR.

      Tel: (020) 8741 8088

5.   *Countrywide Property Auctions*
      144 New London Road,
      Chelmsford, Essex, CM2 0AW.

      Tel: (0870) 240 1140

6.   *Drivers & Norris*
      407 Holloway Road, London,
      N7 6HP.

      Tel: (020) 7607 5001

7.   *Edwin Evans*
      253 Lavender Hill, London,
      SW11 1JW.

      Tel: (020) 7228 5864

8.   *FPD Savills London*
      139 Sloane Street, London,
      SW1X 9AY.

      Tel: (020) 7730 0822

9.   *FPD Savills Nottingham*
      4 St Peters Gate, Nottingham,
      NG1 2JG.

      Tel: (0115) 934 8000

10.   *Halifax Property Services*

      Tel: (0115) 982 9740

11.   *Harman Healy*
      10 Queen Anne Street, London,
      W1G 9LH.

      Tel: (020) 7299 7300

12.   *Keith Pattinson Ltd*
      210 High Street, Gosforth,

      Newcastle Upon Tyne, Tyne And
      Wear, NE3 1HH.

      Tel: 0191 2130550

13.   *McHugh & Co.*
      71 Parkway, Regents Park,
      London, NW1 7PP.

      Tel: (020) 7485 0112

14.   *Nelson Bakewell*
      25, Sackville Street, London,
      W1S 3HQ.

      Tel: (020) 7544 2000

15.   *Pugh & Company*
      Lockside Office Park, Lockside
      Road, Preston, Lancashire,
      PR2 2YS.

      Tel: (01772) 722 444

16.   *Strettons*
      Central House, 189-203 Hoe Street,
      London, E17 3SZ.

      Tel: (020) 8520 9911

17.   *Ward & Partners*
      136 Ashford Road, Bearsted,
      Maidstone, Kent, ME14 4NA.

      Tel: (01622) 730 955

18.   *William H. Brown*
      18-19 Sheep Market, Spalding,
      Lincs, PE11 1BG.

      Tel: (01775) 711 711

19.   *Winkworth & Co.*
      82-84 South End, Croydon, Surrey,
      CR0 1DQ.

      Tel: (020) 8686 6667

xiv) Market appraisals

The author does provide market appraisals on proposed purchases for investors, where he looks at the property details prepared by the estate agent and estimates the likely rental demand and figures. He will then recommend whether you should purchase the property. However, he does not inspect it.

If you are unsure as to whether a property is worth buying, the author can also provide a full written report on the property, which includes an inspection and comments on the investment as a whole. He will then ultimately recommend whether a purchase is worthwhile. For more information, please visit www.spreadtherisk.co.uk.

Glossary

APR	Annual Percentage Rate. This rate is the true cost of borrowing. It takes into account all the fees in obtaining the loan, such as arrangement fees, the actual interest rate on the loan and when the payments are due for the duration of the loan. This avoids mortgage companies misleading the public by quoting a low initial interest rate for the start of the loan and then hitting them with a high interest rate after the initial period. That is why you see adverts for mortgages quoting an attractive initial interest rate and an APR rate. An APR rate has to be quoted in all adverts and publications by law.
ARLA	Association of Residential Letting Agents. A body that regulates letting agents for the letting agents that wish to subscribe to the body. They provide protection for both tenants and landlords.
Arrangement fees	Fees payable to lenders for arranging the mortgage. They can be added to the loan or be paid upon completion.
BOE	Bank of England base rate. This is the interest rate set by the Bank of England in conjunction with the Government to control the economy. Mortgage rates are generally set around this figure.
Capital	This is the amount of money you have personally invested i.e. not borrowed.
Capital appreciation	This is the difference between what you paid for the property and what the property is worth now.
Commission	This is a fee paid to agents based on a percentage of the rental income or selling cost for the services provided by the agent.
Deposit	This is the total money required to obtain the mortgage. This is based as a percentage of the purchase price of the property.

DSS	Department of Social Security. The governmental agency that is responsible for paying out housing benefit to landlords.
Endowment mortgage	A mortgage where you pay the interest on the balance only and then take out an endowment policy to pay the balance of the mortgage at the end of the term of the mortgage. An endowment is a savings scheme where you contribute on a monthly basis and this contribution is invested on the stock market. There is no guarantee that at the end of the term the endowment policy will cover the balance of the mortgage balance.
Equity	The difference between the market value of the house and the borrowings taken out on it.
Exchange of contracts	At this point the buyer and seller are legally bound to transfer ownership. After this, completion occurs usually within one month when all the monies are exchanged.
Freehold	Ownership of a property without time constraint.
Gazumping	This is where the vendor accepts a higher offer from someone else, even though he has accepted an offer already. This is legal if the vendor has not exchanged contracts at the point he has accepted the new offer.
Gazundering	This is where the buyer places another offer lower to the original offer accepted by the vendor prior to exchange of contracts.
Gearing	Gearing an investment simply means borrowing to acquire the investment. The higher the gearing, the higher the borrowing.
Gross yield	This is the annual rental income expressed as a percentage of the total purchase price of the property.
Ground rent	A nominal amount, usually £50, payable to the freeholder due to the ownership of a leasehold.

Guarantor	A guarantor is liable for all debts unpaid by the borrower. A typical guarantor would be a parent of the borrower. So if the son defaults, the lender knows that they can chase the dad for the balance, as he is more likely to be able to pay.
Interest only mortgage	A mortgage where you only pay the interest of the amount borrowed and then settle the balance in full at the end of the mortgage term.
ISA mortgage	Like an endowment mortgage, but the saving scheme is an ISA (Individual Savings Account). This has various tax benefits but has restrictions on total contributions.
LIBOR	London Inter Bank Offered Rate. This is set and fixed quarterly on the first working day of March, June, September and December. It is the average of all the large banks' base rates.
LTV	Loan to value. The loan is expressed as a percentage of the purchase price or valuation. So a loan of £85,000 on a property costing £100,000 is an 85% LTV loan.
Mortgage	A loan that is secured on the property. This means that you own the property, but if you default on the loan the lender can order the property to be sold to recover his debt. Any surpluses arising from the sale are yours.
Negative equity	This is where the mortgage on the property exceeds the market value of the property. The amount it exceeds it by is the amount of negative equity.
Net yield	This is the annual profit expressed as a percentage of the total purchase price of the property. Profit being rental income less mortgage costs and repairs.
Payment in advance	This is where the tenant pays the rent at the start of the period.
Payment in arrears	This is where the tenant pays the rent at the end of the period.

Pension mortgage	Like an endowment mortgage, but the saving scheme is a pension. This has various tax benefits but restrictions on total contributions and the borrower's age at the end of the term.
Profit	All incomes less all expenditure, excluding all asset sales and purchases.
Redemption penalty	The financial penalty that is liable if you were to repay the debt early in full.
Remortgage	This is where you already have a mortgage but wish to change lender. The new lender settles the debt to the existing lender. Remortgaging has two key features: 1. You can obtain a better interest rate (or a rate that suits you, e.g. fixed) that you are currently paying on your existing borrowings by sourcing the most suitable lender on the market. Your existing lender may be uncompetitive or unable to provide the type of mortgage you require. 2. You can raise finance on the increase of value of your property. So, for example, if you own a property that you purchased for £100,000 ten years ago with a £95,000 mortgage which is now worth £200,000, you can remortgage and access the £100,000 increase by getting a mortgage for say £190,000, releasing £95,000.
Repayment mortgage	A mortgage where you pay the interest and the capital over the duration of the mortgage. This type of mortgage ensures that you pay off the mortgage at the end of the term.
Repossession	Repossession occurs when the borrower defaults on the mortgage and the lender has legally to enforce the sale of the property to recover its debt.
Return	Same as gross yield.

Secured loan	The term secured means that the lender is 'secured' to get payment on the loan if the borrower defaults. The loan is only granted if you can supply sufficient security, typically being a house or car. If you default, the lender can repossess the security, sell it on the open market and recover their debt.
Service charge	The charge paid to service the property on which you have a lease on. The service charge is a proportion of the total repairs and maintenance costs in the year.
Title deeds	Legal documents that show the legal ownership of the property.
Under offer	A property that has an offer accepted by the vendor but the vendor and the purchaser have not exchanged contracts.
Unsecured loan	A loan where no security has been offered by the borrower to the lender. The lender has only the courts to go to if the borrower defaults to enforce payment.

Index

A

accommodation projects 18-19, 29
    information 92-106
advertising 48
    information in 29-30
    by letting agents 30
    as research 20
    for tenants 29-30, 39
appreciation, capital 18 *see also*
                investments
ARLA (Association of Residential Letting
    Agents) 36, 127
ASTs (Assured Shorthold Tenancies)
          52, 57
    Agreement, template 53-6
auctioneers 129-30
auctions
    bidding 25
    deposits 25
    guide prices 23
    information 24, 25
    practice runs 23
    vs private sales 24
    purchases
        as contracts 24, 25
        conditions 25
        funding 24
        solicitors 24, 25, 26
    readiness 23, 24-5
    surveys 24-5
    viewing for 24
    withdrawals at 26

B

banks, rent collection by 36-7
bathrooms 20
bedrooms 20, 30
bidding, auctions 25
borrowing *see* funding
buildings insurance 58

C

capital appreciation 18 *see also*
              investments
capital assets 49
Capital Gains Tax 45
    gains basis 9, 47, 49
    minimising 50
cashback on completion 9-10
CCJs (County Court Judgments) 13
CIFAS (Credit Industry Fraud Avoidance
    System) 13
claw-backs 34
commercial properties, dwellings above 12
condition of properties 20-1
construction, non-standard, properties 12
contact details 30
    low-cost, providers 125
contents insurance 58
contracts
    auction purchases as 24, 25
    for funding 51
    for insurance 58, 126
    with letting agents 59

The Buy-to-Let Bible

market appraisals 131

mortgage brokers, information 91

mortgages 6

    auction purchases 24

    buy-to-let

        anonymity 14-15

        and creditworthiness 13

        deposits 11

        and first investments 11-12

        interest rates and risks 14

        lock-in periods 14

        profiling by 15

        providers 67-89

        and purchase prices 12

        tailored 11, 15

    delays 22

    100% fee-free 7

        providers 63-7

    remortgages 41-2, 43

motivation ix, 7

motoring costs 48

multi-storey properties 12

multi-title properties 12

N

NICEIC (National Inspection Council for Electrical Installation) contractors 60

O

offers

    interpersonal skills in 21

    readiness 21

    threats to 22-3

P

partners, financial, funding by 7

payback periods 17

portfolios, building, by equity release 41-2

post, rent by 38

press, local 29-30, 129

prices *see* guide prices; rent

purchase prices

    control of 17

    vs locations 17-18

    and mortgages 11-12

    valuations to 9

R

refurbishment 19, 38

    see also repairs

remortgages 41-2, 43

rent 32

    collection

        by banks 36-7

        convenience factors 35

        by letting agents 35-6

        in person 38

        by post 38

    DSS tenants 34

    ground rent 48

    guaranteed 126

    increases 42

    reductions 30-1

    taxable 45-6

    as wear-and-tear allowance 49

repairs 46

    insurance for 58

    see also refurbishment

responsible attitudes xi, 19, 59-60

retirement relief 50

142

W

wear-and-tear allowances 49

wiring 21

withdrawals

       at auctions 25-6

       by vendor 22

Y

yields, gross 17-19 *see also* investments

More books available from Lawpack...

Harry Greene's Complete DIY Problem Solver

Harry Greene is the doyen of DIY, whose career in TV DIY broadcasting spans - unbelievably - half a century. In this milestone, full-colour book, published to coincide with Harry's 50 years on TV, he reveals not only his great skill as a communicator and illustrator, but also his encyclopedic and unparalleled knowledge of problem-solving DIY practices and techniques, built up over a lifetime of infectious enthusiam for the subject.

Code B441	ISBN 1 904053 28 9		Hardback
280 x 220mm	320pp	£19.99	1st edition

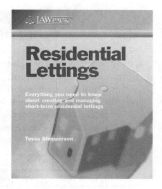

Residential Lettings

Are you thinking of letting a flat or a house? This guide steers anyone who intends - or already is - letting property through the legal and practical issues involved. It provides all the up-to-date information and tips that a would-be landlord needs. It will also alert existing landlords to the points of good practice that make a letting successful, and the legal obligations that they may not be aware of. For lettings in England & Wales and Scotland.

Code B422	ISBN 1 904053 34 3		PB
245 x 199mm	112pp	£11.99	3rd edition

Buying Bargains at Property Auctions

Every week, hundreds of commercial and residential properties are sold at auction in Britain, often at bargain prices, with owner-occupiers accounting for a growing proportion of buyers. In this bestselling guide, author and property auctioneer Howard Gooddie spells out how straightforward the auction route can be and divulges the tips and practices of this relatively unknown world.

Code B426	ISBN 1 904053 37 8		PB
245 x 199mm	168pp	£11.99	2nd edition

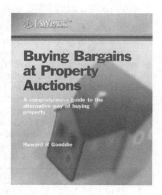

To order, visit www.lawpack.co.uk or call 020 7394 4040

More books available from Lawpack...

Employment Law

Whether you are an employer or an employee, you have ever-increasing rights and duties in the workplace. This bestselling guide, by specialist solicitor Melanie Hunt, is a comprehensive source of up-to-date knowledge on hiring, wages, employment contracts, family-friendly rights, discrimination, termination and other important issues. It puts at your fingertips the important legal points that all employers and employees should know about.

Code B408	ISBN 1 904053 30 0	PB	
240 x 167mm	192pp	£11.99	6th edition

Separation & Divorce

Separation and divorce do not have to be very costly and difficult. This guide gives you the instructions and information you need to manage your own divorce, without the expense of a solicitor. It explains the legal and financial issues involved, and takes you step-by-step from the petition to the final decree. For use in England & Wales.

Code B445	ISBN 1 904053 32 7	PB	
240 x 167mm	160pp	£11.99	1st edition

Wills, Power of Attorney & Probate

Who will manage your property if you can't do it yourself? Who will inherit it on your death? And what must your executors do then? This guide covers these key questions and explains the steps you can take. With a power of attorney, you can authorise someone to act on your behalf with legal authority; in a Will, you appoint executors and give instructions about whom you wish to inherit your property; and via probate, executors gain authority to handle the assets of an estate and administer a Will after death. For use in England & Wales and Scotland.

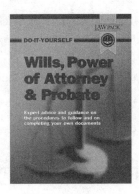

Code B407	ISBN 1 904053 33 5	PB	
240 x 167mm	248pp	£11.99	1st edition

To order, visit www.lawpack.co.uk or call 020 7394 4040

More books available from Lawpack...

Legal Advice Handbook

Where do you go for legal advice? As the sources of both free and paid-for legal advice become more diverse and specific areas of law demand greater specialisation from the advice givers, the need for a consumer guide to this expanding, unmapped network has never been greater. Solicitor Tessa Shepperson has gathered together extensive research data and produced an invaluable handbook.

Code B427	ISBN 1 902646 71 1	PB
A5	192pp	£7.99	1st edition

How to Complain Effectively

Faulty goods, shoddy service, poor advice... these are things most of us, at some time, feel we have good reason to complain about. In this practical guide, Steve Wiseman draws on his extensive experience as a Citizens Advice Bureau manager and tells you how to ensure your complaint has maximum impact, whether it be against your local shop or a government department.

Code B430	ISBN 1 902646 80 0	PB
A5	160pp	£7.99	1st edition

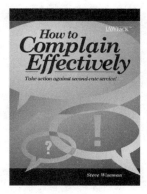

Tax Answers at a Glance

With the emphasis on self-assessment, we all need to have a hold on the array of taxes now levied by government. Compiled by tax experts and presented in question-and-answer format, this handy guide provides a useful summary of Income Tax, VAT, Capital Gains Tax, Inheritance Tax, pensions, self-employment, partnerships, land and property, trusts and estates, Corporation Tax, stamp duty and more. For 2003/04 tax year.

Code B425	ISBN 1 904053 84 3	PB
A5	192pp	£7.99	3rd edition

To order, visit www.lawpack.co.uk or call 020 7394 4040